W9-BXV-717

"May You
SHINE *your* LIGHT
and be a beacon
to others!

Love,

Cynthia Mazzaferro
2017

SHINE *your* LIGHT

*Powerful Practices
for an Extraordinary Life*

New York Times Bestselling Authors,

Janet Bray Attwood
Marci Shimoff
Chris Attwood
with Geoff Affleck

and 26 Transformational Leaders:
Keiko Anaguchi, Ronica Arnold Branson, Jannie Bak,
Markeita L. Banya, Alison Braithwaite, Jim Claussen, Ramon G. Corrales,
Jennifer Dean, Dipika Delmenico, Ron Holt, Jeanette Jardine,
Debra Kelsey-Davis, Michele Bray MacNair, Helgi Maki, Cynthia Mazzaferro,
Lisa McDonald, Carol McNulty-Huffman, Maru Méndez, Susan Mercer,
Guillermo Paz, Linda Solberg, Kirsten Stendevad, John Tolmie,
Pia Nissen Tylak, Magnes Welsh, Lori Woodley

NEW YORK

NASHVILLE • MELBOURNE • VANCOUVER

SHINE *your* LIGHT
Powerful Practices for an Extraordinary Life

© 2018 Janet Bray Attwood, Marci Shimoff, Chris Attwood with Geoff Affleck

All rights reserved. No portion of this book may be reproduced, stored in a retrieval system, or transmitted in any form or by any means—electronic, mechanical, photocopy, recording, scanning, or other,—except for brief quotations in critical reviews or articles, without the prior written permission of the publisher.

Published in New York, New York, by Morgan James Publishing. Morgan James is a trademark of Morgan James, LLC. www.MorganJamesPublishing.com

The Morgan James Speakers Group can bring authors to your live event. For more information or to book an event visit The Morgan James Speakers Group at www.TheMorganJamesSpeakersGroup.com.

ISBN 978-1-68350-545-7 paperback
ISBN 978-1-68350-546-4 eBook
Library of Congress Control Number: 2017905728

Compiled by:
Geoff Affleck
www.geoffaffleck.com

Edited by:
Cindy Buck

Proofreading by:
Page Two
www.pagetwostrategies.com

Cover Design by:
Rachel Lopez
www.r2cdesign.com

Interior Design by:
Bonnie Bushman
The Whole Caboodle Graphic Design

In an effort to support local communities, raise awareness and funds, Morgan James Publishing donates a percentage of all book sales for the life of each book to Habitat for Humanity Peninsula and Greater Williamsburg.

Get involved today! Visit
www.MorganJamesBuilds.com

We dedicate this book to our families, friends and colleagues who have supported our journeys. Knowing that there are no mistakes in the Universe, it is our joy to offer these stories, tools and words of wisdom to those who have been drawn to these pages..

Contents

Chapter 1

The Transforming Power of Letting Go
Janet Bray Attwood

Have you ever let go of it all? The most remarkable things can happen when you surrender completely.

Letting go and trusting in the universe is probably the all-time greatest challenge anyone can face. We walk in the dark with total blind faith, not knowing where the next safe footing will be, afraid that the unknown will unveil more than we can take. And yet, I've learned that the key to living a happy, fulfilled life is to become completely comfortable with "not knowing" what will come next.

In 1980, I had my first dramatic experience of consciously handing my life over to the universe. I was recruiting disk-drive engineers in Silicon Valley and failing miserably. Luckily for me, one day after work when I was meditating in the local meditation center, I opened my eyes and glanced upon a sign on the bulletin board that advertised a success seminar called "Yes to Success" to be held in San Francisco the following weekend. All circuits firing, I knew that somehow the answer to my prayers had everything to do with taking that seminar.

If you've read my book *The Passion Test*, then you know my intuition couldn't have been more right on. Not only did I take the seminar, but I eventually persuaded the seminar leader, a vivacious and passionate woman named Debra Poneman, to hire me. As luck would have it, Debra was going on her U.S. speaking tour at the same time I was to arrive in Los Angeles, where her company was located, and she needed someone to housesit. She said I could stay in her apartment, study her success tapes while she was gone and, when she returned, I could start my illustrious career, uplifting and speaking to hundreds of people all over the world.

I was in seventh heaven!

Two weeks later, after Debra and I finalized our plans, I said good-bye to all my friends at the recruiting firm, packed my bags, filled up my vintage red Toyota with gas and headed down to Los Angeles, radio blaring, singing at the top of my lungs, ecstatic that I was on my way to start my dream career.

Two miles into my journey, my red Toyota started sputtering and spurting. Steam was rising up over the front of my car from inside the hood. As I was pulling over to the side of the freeway to see what was going on, my trusty little car took one big breath, let out the most god-awful sound and died.

Horrified, I just sat there, frozen, on the side of the freeway, stunned at what had just happened.

After the initial shock of losing my beloved Toyota, I came up with an alternate plan. I'd take a train down to Los Angeles. After paying the tow truck, buying my train ticket to Los Angeles and then taking a long taxi ride to Debra's apartment in Santa Monica, to my dismay and alarm, I arrived at Debra's door with $13 to my name.

As a little girl, I had dreamed of being an actress, performing in front of thousands of people. Well, this performance was only for one person, but it required all my acting skills. I was terrified that Debra wouldn't hire me to go out and teach other people her success principles if she knew I was completely broke. So, I said nothing while we were together and kept a sunny smile on my face until she finally waved good-bye to me.

The good news was that Debra had let me stay in her apartment. The not-so-good news was that I had no money to buy food or anything else!

Now what am I going to do? I thought to myself. Feeling totally weighed down by the fact that I hardly had enough money to last me more than a few days, I went to Debra's refrigerator and scooped myself a huge serving of her chocolate ice cream. After eating almost the whole half gallon, I lay down on her couch and fell into a drunken chocolate sleep.

When I awoke, I decided there was only one option when things were this bad.

I grabbed the keys to Debra's blue Chevy (she'd said I could borrow it for emergencies—this was clearly an emergency) and headed down the Pacific Coast Highway with a renewed sense of hope. When all is lost, what can you lose by giving it all up?

Arriving at the great saint Paramahansa Yogananda's Self-Realization Fellowship Lake Shrine in Pacific Palisades, I immediately felt a deep sense of calm come over me. I walked past all of the beautiful buildings to the majestic and serene gardens that graced this special place.

Reaching into my purse, I pulled out my treasured, crisp one-dollar bills and stuffed all $13 into a little wooden donation box that was located in the garden.

When I had given away all I had, I sat down on a nearby wooden bench and had a very intimate talk with God, pouring out my heart. I told Him all that was going on with me and where I could use a little of His support.

After a little while, I walked back to Debra's car as the reality of what I'd done began to dawn. As I drove back to Debra's, the self-recrimination began: *Are you crazy? What are you going to do now? How could you give away the last money you have in the world? Now you don't even have money to buy lunch!*

As I opened the door to Debra's apartment, the phone rang.

"Hello," I said.

"Janet, is that you?"

"Uh huh. Who's this?" I asked.

"It's me, Patrick."

Patrick was my ex-husband's father, who I completely loved and hadn't heard from in over a year.

"Hi, Patrick. It's so nice to hear from you. How did you find me?" I asked.

After we chatted on the phone for some time, he invited me to meet him for lunch at a nearby restaurant. Of course I accepted, thinking, *Thank you, God! No matter what happens, at least I'll have a meal in my belly.*

Patrick was unbelievably animated and talking 100 miles a minute. He had just started selling a natural weight-loss program he was really excited about. He put four bottles of the stuff on the table and said this was just the beginning for me.

"Janet," he said, "I think, if you want to, this is something you could really make a lot of money on in your spare time." He knew that I have an outgoing personality and love to share things I think are great with other people.

Patrick still had that same sparkle in his eyes I had always loved, and when he spoke about the products he had set down before me, I couldn't help but start to feel excited about it, too.

"The opportunity sounds great," I said. "How about when I have some extra money, I'll order some from you?"

"I don't think you should wait that long," Patrick said to me, smiling. "I just happen to have five hundred dollars' worth of the stuff in the trunk of my car. You can have these bottles on the table and the five hundred dollars' worth as well. Pay me back after you sell it all and make some money for yourself."

Just as he handed over the four bottles, our very overweight waitress walked up to the table and said to me, "What's that?"

I told her everything I could remember that Patrick had just told me. These were wonderful, all-natural products, so many people had had great experiences losing weight with them, and they were easy to use.

"I'll take everything you have!" she said and immediately whipped out a $100 bill from her apron, grabbed the bottles and walked away.

I sat there stunned and overjoyed. Thanking Patrick as we said good-bye, I headed home.

This experience was a profound lesson for me. One which I've remembered often during the 36 years since these events took place.

We're always taken care of. Donating my last $13 was my way of surrendering to that force, which is always looking after us. I learned that all that's required of me is to let go of my agenda and surrender to God's will for me.

When you do that, the result is always better than what you could have come up with on your own.

Having said that, please don't go out and donate all your possessions to charity, unless you feel an irresistible pull to do that and are fully prepared to live with the consequences. Surrender means being willing to welcome whatever life has in store for you.

Your safety valve is your passions—the things you love and care about most. When you're connected to those things, then you can be assured that your life will grow increasingly meaningful and fulfilling.

When we give The Passion Test, we always share the one secret that guarantees a passionate life: "Whenever you're faced with a choice, a decision or an opportunity, choose in favor of your passions."

But there's a stumbling block many people trip over on their way to creating the life of their dreams: their own thoughts.

"What you see you become" is a quote from a Vedic text from ancient India. It doesn't mean that when you see a donkey, you become a donkey. It means that what you perceive is filtered through the thoughts you have about that thing. Your thoughts, your beliefs and the concepts and ideas you hold about your life are what determine how you experience life.

You see, your life can be filled with miracles—just like my experience of giving away my last $13—if you believe it can. Your life can also be a tragedy, if that's what you believe it is.

You can create miracles in your life by strengthening your belief that miracles are possible. Before you give away your last dollar, find the evidence that miracles can happen. Your mind is a wonderful machine. If you give it enough evidence that something is possible, it will become possible for you.

So, let me give you some evidence of the possibility of miracles when you learn to choose in favor of your passions, the things that matter most to you, by telling you one of my favorite Chris stories. (By the way, if you don't know what your passions are, get a copy of *The Passion Test* at www.passiontest.com—it's a simple way to quickly clarify your passions.)

Chris Attwood, co-author of *The Passion Test,* and I had spoken at one of Jack Canfield's advanced seminars and were on our way home via the Los Angeles airport. After we had dropped off our rental car and the shuttle that had taken us to the airport pulled away from the curb, Chris suddenly realized he was missing one of his bags with all his clothes in it. Unable to catch the shuttle, he spent the next 40 minutes calling the rental car company, stopping every shuttle from the rental car company that came by and doing everything he could think of to get his suitcase back.

Finally, the time came when he had to either get on the plane or stay and wait for his suitcase. It was time to either "fish or cut bait" when it came to following his passions.

So, Chris asked himself, *Does staying in L.A. and waiting for my suitcase help me be more aligned with my passions, or will it take me farther away from living those passions?*

One of Chris's passions is having fun with everything he does. He had a teleconference to lead that evening. If he stayed in L.A., he would have to look not only for his suitcase but also for someplace where he could set up his computer and conduct that teleconference. It didn't sound like much fun to him.

Another of his top passions is living a life of abundance on every level. When he thought about which option made him feel more abundant—waiting around the L.A. airport and searching for someplace to do his teleconference, or having a leisurely trip home without worrying about his suitcase—the choice was clear.

As he came up to the gate, I was overjoyed. "I knew you would find your suitcase!" I exclaimed. "I didn't," Chris replied, and then we both started laughing.

We had a fun trip home and Chris led a great teleconference that night. The next day, Continental Airlines called to say, "The police dropped off a suitcase here with your name on it. What would you like us to do with it?"

"Could you put it on a plane to San Francisco for me?" Chris asked. After checking, the agent came back on the line and said, "No problem." A few hours later Chris had his suitcase.

Now, this certainly doesn't count as a major miracle, but it's a wonderful small one. And this story illustrates several points that are key to living a passionate life and creating the kind of life you really choose to live:

- **Your thoughts/beliefs can make you happy or miserable.** Chris believed that it was more important to have fun and feel abundant than to worry about his suitcase. As a result, he had fun and he felt abundant. As an added bonus (and this is common when you follow your passions), he got his suitcase back without effort or strain.

- **You can't know the outcome—it's all about surrender.** Your beliefs and thoughts affect how you experience anything in your life ("what you see you become"), but you can never know what specific outcomes will occur. This is why following your passions is so important. No matter what the result, you will be in the flow of life. Just as I had no idea what would happen when I donated my last $13, Chris had no idea whether he would ever see his suitcase again when he made his decision to go home.

- **Staying open is one of the keys to living a passionate life.** Because you can't know the outcome, staying open to what is appearing is absolutely essential. When you are open, then you're ready to welcome the unexpected gifts that will show up in your life.

- **Following your passions takes courage.** Because you have to make the decision to follow your passion when you don't know what the outcome will be, you have to make a leap of faith. When Chris decided to leave his suitcase behind to follow his passions, he had to be prepared to never see that suitcase again. When I gave away my last $13, I had to be prepared to accept whatever came.

In *The Passion Test*, we tell my story of my passion to go to India and interview the enlightened, and how I gave it all up to be with my dying stepmother. I had to make that decision with the knowledge that I might never be able to fulfill my passion to do those interviews. Of course, as it turned out, it was being with my stepmother that was key to being able to follow that passion.

Don't fall for the myth that the world is an "objective" reality that you can't change. This is an illusion that leads to feeling like a victim. And guess what, if you believe you're a victim of your circumstances, you will be. Funny how that works.

Change your beliefs about what you experience and you will change your life. You are powerful. It's now up to you to claim your power.

Janet Bray Attwood is a visionary, a transformational leader and a world humanitarian. She is co-author of the New York Times *bestsellers,* The Passion Test: The Effortless Path to Discovering Your Life Purpose *and* Your Hidden Riches: Unleashing the Power of Ritual to Create a Life of Meaning and Purpose. *Janet has trained almost 2,000 certified Passion Test facilitators in more than 60 countries.*

Janet has spoken about how to discover passion and purpose throughout the world and has shared the stage with His Holiness the 14th Dalai Lama, Dr. Stephen Covey, Richard Branson, Nobel Peace Prize–winner F.W. de Klerk, Jack Canfield, Zappo's CEO Tony Hsieh, Reverend Michael Beckwith and many others. She is also a founding member of the Transformational Leadership Council.

For her ongoing work with homeless women and youth in lockdown detention centers, Janet received the highest award for volunteer service in the U.S., the President's Volunteer Service Award.

Janet is a living example of what it means to live with an open heart and mind. Learn more at www.thepassiontest.com.

Chapter 2

Two Big Mistakes That May Be
Keeping You from Living a Miraculous Life

Marci Shimoff

One glorious morning recently, I woke up in a beautiful resort in Costa Rica. My day overflowed with miracles. I was there at a meeting of the Transformational Leadership Council, a group of 125 of the top transformational leaders in the world, founded by one of my mentors, Jack Canfield.

As I ate my breakfast on the veranda overlooking the crystal blue ocean and attended the meetings filled with wisdom, laughter and deep connections, and then ended the day with a gorgeous sunset dinner cruise, I thought, *It doesn't get much better than this.* And I go to these meetings twice every year at magical and exotic locations around the world…

Yes, my life feels miraculous—but it certainly wasn't always that way. Not by a long shot.

In fact, if you had told me that I would someday wake up every morning feeling like I live a miraculous life, I would have said you were crazy.

You see, I was born depressed. Even though I was blessed with a wonderful, loving family and comfortable circumstances, I was not a happy camper throughout my childhood and teen years—I felt like I had a dark cloud around me.

I continued to feel unhappy in my 20s, 30s and early 40s, even though wealth, recognition and fame came to me during those years. I worked hard to fill my life with success and what I thought I needed to be happy, only to find myself still feeling empty at my core. I was exhausted, and I walked around every day with a physical pain in my heart that no doctor could explain or "cure."

It was only when I began studying the science of happiness and applying what I learned to my daily life that everything turned around. By the time I was 50, I was genuinely happy and my heart pain had gone away on its own—honestly, that seemed like a miracle to me.

But then something even more wonderful happened. I began to notice that everything in my life felt like it was "in the flow." The right people were showing up at just the right time, whatever I needed was appearing out of nowhere, and a sense of ease and happiness was growing in my heart. Wow, was that nice! Miracles seemed to be happening almost every day.

So, I decided to do some research on living a miraculous life, and what I discovered was thrilling: there are simple steps anyone can take to start living in that miracle flow.

While we can't create miracles, we can create the conditions for miracles to flow in our lives. That's what I call "Living in the Miracle Zone."

And that's what I teach in the program called "Your Year of Miracles" that I created with my dear friend, transformational teacher Debra Poneman. Together, we've discovered the biggest mistakes that keep people from living a miraculous life, and I want to share the two biggest ones with you now. When you understand these common mistakes and what to do about them, you will find yourself living in the Miracle Zone more and more every day.

Mistake #1: Holding On When It's Time to Let Go

At some point in your life, you have to simply let go of the past…whether it's letting go of a job where you feel like you're dying a slow death, a business that no longer brings you any kind of fulfillment, a relationship that was really over years ago or an expensive piece of jewelry that was given to you by your former mother-in-law.

When you let go, you create space for something infinitely better to come into your life.

So why do we make the mistake of holding on? There's only one reason: fear. We think things like…

What if I let go of this job and then the management changes, and this company becomes a wonderful place to work?

I don't love my husband, but at least I have a roof over my head.

What if I get rid of this jacket and then can't find another one to replace it?

Really? Is that how you want to live your life?

You hold on to things out of fear that something better won't come and take their place. But I promise you, something will come. And you know what that something is?

Miracles.

In order to allow miracles into your life, you have to make space for them by letting go of what no longer serves you. On all levels in your life, you have to clear out old energy, objects, beliefs and sometimes people, so you can make space for the new.

When you let go of what's not working, you're basically saying to the Universe, "I know you have my back, so I'm going to let go and trust that there's something better on its way for me."

So, start letting go of stuff. For many, it's easiest to start on the most superficial level and get rid of the physical clutter in your environment. Once that stuff starts to move, your energy is freed up, and letting go of the bigger things—old habits, self-limiting beliefs, unsupportive relationships that don't serve you—becomes easier.

Everything we own carries a charge of energy with it. It's amazing how letting go of something as seemingly innocuous as old pots and pans can help start the momentum that allows us to get a whole new kitchen, house or partner! So don't think the physical world of objects is too superficial a place to start.

I recommend a simple feng shui ritual designed to help you let go. If you want a fresh start and new energy in your life, I invite you to try this: each day for nine days in a row, give away, throw away or somehow eliminate from your home or office 27 items—that's right, 27 items a day for nine days.

These items can be clothes you've kept for years (just in case you get back to a size 6!), chipped dishes, spoons dinged up by the garbage disposal, knickknacks accumulating dust—and they can also be your unfaithful boyfriend and your habit of staying up too late watching TV. Look for whatever no longer serves you.

Here are some guidelines:

1. If you skip a day, you have to start over with Day 1 because the energy is cumulative.
2. If you're not sure about an item, hold it to your heart and ask, "Does this represent my ideal self in the future?"
3. Get rid of books, tapes and CDs you won't use again.
4. Toss outdated food, vitamins, old medicines and broken appliances.
5. Give away or toss anything that holds an unpleasant memory.
6. Examine your feelings and see if you're holding on to resentments, hurts or guilt. Acknowledge the feeling and ask it to leave now.
7. Does someone in your life always make you feel bad about yourself? There's no law against deciding to see someone less, or not at all, if they aren't having a positive effect on your life.
8. As you let go, thank the item, emotion or relationship warmly for its previous usefulness, and then say good-bye to it with gratitude in your heart.

After the nine days, see if what's left truly represents who you are now and who you intend to be in the future.

It's a law of physics that "nature abhors a vacuum." So, when you create space, the Universe rushes in to fill it up. When you release old relationships that no longer work, new and more wonderful ones have space to come in. When you let go of old resentments, more loving energy can enter. When you let go of the items in your home that carry old energy, more appropriate things will come in. You'll see that miracles will fill those empty spaces faster than you can say, "I love living in the Miracle Zone!"

Mistake #2: Not Thinking You're Worthy of Miracles

Maybe you don't think you deserve to live a miraculous life. Well, the truth is that the miracles you most want also want you. They're eager for you to love yourself enough to feel worthy of them and let them in.

Now, you've probably heard it said that no one can love you more than you love yourself, and people can only give you what you're willing to give yourself. It's the same with the Universe—it will only give you what you feel worthy of. Until you develop deep self-love, it's going to be hard for those miracles to show up.

So, how do you know if you have self-love? Well, one way to tell is that you feel content, regardless of your circumstances. Another is, you don't depend on someone else's love in order to feel good about yourself. If you find it easy to let others love you, you probably have a good amount of self-love.

And self-love is different than self-esteem. Self-esteem is conditional: *I love myself because I'm smart, or because I'm attractive or caring.* But that "because" makes the love conditional. Self-esteem is something that you earn. But self-love is an unconditional experience of love for yourself, no matter what's going on. It doesn't depend on you being smart or pretty or talented or even a loving person. It doesn't depend on you being anything. It's about an unconditional acceptance of yourself, no matter what!

Self-esteem is great, but it's really self-love you need in order to live in the Miracle Zone. When you don't have self-love, you block the miracles because you don't feel worthy of them. Unconsciously, you push them away on an energetic level.

No matter who we are, all of us were wounded in some way or another when we were children. Some of us were abused physically and some of us were abused emotionally. Maybe you were neglected. Maybe your parents inadvertently and unknowingly hurt you by minimizing the sadness or fear you tried to express.

Something happened to all of us. In fact, multiple things happened to all of us. And we created false beliefs around those incidents by interpreting them through the mind of our childhood self.

In reality, what happened may have had little or nothing to do with our interpretation of those events, yet we've been living our lives as if those false beliefs were true. They may be things like *I am alone* or *I'm bad* or *I'm never enough* or *I'm too much* or *I'm not wanted* or *I'm not safe.*

Let me share a very personal story from my own life that created a core belief that I'm not wanted.

My mother, in all innocence, loved to tell this story frequently because she felt it was actually a wonderful tale with a positive ending. But it had the opposite effect on me.

My brother and sister are 10 and 11 years older than I am, respectively. From what I understand, they were a total handful growing up, often at each other's throats, and my mother used to say that it was too much for her. She would tell her friends that if she ever got pregnant again, she would just drive off into the ocean.

Well, sure enough, she did get pregnant again—with me—and the way she told the story is that she was so happy she didn't drive off into the ocean. She would add just how wonderful I am and end the story with "Honey, you may not have been wanted, but you were always loved."

Yes, it's a lovely message, but what I heard above all else is that *I may not have been wanted*—and I could not own the part that I was always loved. Every time my mother told the story, which was regularly (even the week before she passed away at the age of 88), all I could hear was that I wasn't wanted.

That's how I developed a false core belief about myself, and it's shown up in many ways in my life, including in my personal relationships, in my relationship with myself and in my work. For most of my life, I felt that I had to prove myself because, inherently, I didn't feel wanted for who I was. That meant I had to create some amazing value in order for people to want me.

As I've become more aware of this pattern and done healing processes (one of which I'm about to share with you), I've been able to dissolve that limiting belief. I no longer believe it's true, and releasing it has freed up my life. I'm willing to put myself out there much more because I feel wanted for me, for who I am, and, most importantly, *I* want me! I don't have to prove myself anymore.

Here's a technique I find very powerful when I'm feeling a lack of self-love, unworthiness or any kind of emotional pain:

1. Allow your attention to scan your body and locate where you're feeling a sensation that wants your attention. Emotional discomfort of any kind is somewhere in the body, as well as in your mind. Whether it's tightness in the throat, pressure in the chest or contraction in the gut, that feeling tells you where your body is holding the emotion.

2. Place your hand on your body where the feeling is located and take a few deep breaths into that feeling. And then send it love. You can even say to it, "Thank you. I love you." This will allow it to begin to unwind.

3. As this process continues, the sensation will usually decrease. In some cases, it might increase as it's leaving your body. To aid the healing process, you might want to do something physical, like dance or do yoga or take a warm bath.

4. Whatever direction the sensation takes, it has a message for you. Even a sensation that you might label as pain is really a portal to healing and wisdom. Ask what the message is. Sometimes it's very clear. Sometimes it might be a reminder that you have the power to heal yourself, to dissolve old wounds, to love yourself into a state of wellness and to restore yourself to a state of wholeness. Maybe that pain is a gift, and when you open it by putting your attention on it, you'll discover that you are not only worthy of being well and whole but, truly, you are worthy of miracles.

When you have let go of what's not useful to you, and let in the belief that you are worthy of what you truly want, you will start to live the life of your dreams. You will wake up each morning in the flow and watch everything unfold with more ease than ever before—no matter what life throws your way.

That's the promise of life in the Miracle Zone.

Marci Shimoff is a #1 New York Times *bestselling author, a world-renowned transformational teacher and an expert on happiness, success and unconditional love. Her books include the international bestsellers* Love for No Reason *and* Happy for No Reason. *Marci is also the woman's face of the biggest self-help book phenomenon in history, as co-author of six books in the* Chicken Soup for the Woman's Soul *series. With total book sales of more than 15 million copies worldwide in 33 languages, Marci is one of the bestselling female nonfiction authors of all time.*

Marci is also a featured teacher in the hit film and book, The Secret, *and the host of the national PBS TV show called* Happy for No Reason. *She delivers keynote speeches and seminars on happiness and empowerment.*

Along with her dedication to helping people live more empowered and joy-filled lives, Marci's current passion is mentoring people in her program Your Year of Miracles. She can be reached at www.HappyforNoReason.com and www.YourYearOfMiracles.com.

Chapter 3

Solving the Puzzle of Life
Chris Attwood

I n February 1970, I walked out of a lecture, crossed the green, open soccer fields on my way home and counted 17 police cars streaming into my little student community of Isla Vista, next to UC Santa Barbara in California. I'll tell you what happened in a moment, but first let's talk about you.

We're each dropped into a gigantic puzzle when we're born. Your job here is to solve that puzzle. No one can do it for you; you have to solve the puzzle for yourself. Yet we can learn from each other and, in doing so, get clues to the solution to our own puzzle.

As you solve your puzzle, you begin to discover success and harmony in each area of your life. When you solve the puzzle of finances, you begin to enjoy financial comfort. When you solve the puzzle of relationships, you begin to enjoy a loving, connected relationship. When you solve the puzzle of consciousness itself, you become at ease in any situation with any outcome, neither attracted to nor repulsed by anything. Mine has been a meandering journey. I share my story in the hope it will help you find the solution to your puzzle and create a life grounded in fulfillment.

That evening, after those police cars streamed into Isla Vista, I stood on a street corner with 3,000 others, watching as the Bank of America in the center of town—a monstrosity of a building—was set on fire. The police sent in a bus of 50 officers in full riot gear to make sure no one was in the burning bank. They marched across the open field and arranged themselves in front of the crowd.

Some of them looked scared. Some looked angry as they held their wooden batons and their plastic shields, their heads covered with helmets. On the other side, many of the young people yelled epithets at the police, throwing rocks and bottles. There was a great deal of emotion on both sides, but love was not one of those emotions.

At some point the commander in charge of the police decided the young people were getting too close, and he ordered the officers to charge the crowd. They swung their billy clubs and, in some cases, hit students lying on the ground again and again.

Three times they charged.

Each time, the crowd got angrier and angrier. Finally, with a collective cry of rage, those 3,000 students rushed the police. The officers turned and ran as fast as they could back across the field and onto their bus.

The Bank of America burned to the ground that night. But it was a victory for no one. As I watched that night and again two more times that year as riots erupted in Isla Vista, hundreds were injured or imprisoned, and one student was mistakenly shot to death by police. What I saw was anger and hate, from all sides, fueled into a frenzy that ripped us apart.

The first big puzzle piece fell into place for me: this is not the kind of world I choose to live in, and I'm going to do what I can to change it.

Motivated by the events on that fateful evening, I committed myself to creating a new way of living in the world. Being 21 years old, I thought, *If we can just create models of new institutions that encourage cooperation and mutual support, then those models can be expanded all over, and we can create a new world!*

So, I joined the community development effort that emerged after the riots of 1970. We created barrier parks to reduce auto traffic and beautify our community. We got empty lots designated as parks and then planted trees and flowers. We arranged for students to be able to ride the buses just by showing their student IDs, and we even got the county planning commission to rezone our community so it could become more livable.

As part of this effort, I was one of the founders of the Isla Vista Füd Co-op (F-U-D stood for "fucked-up dopers," and the "ü" was chosen to make it sound like "food"). We got 1,000 people, 10 percent of the whole community, to join the Co-op and agree to volunteer one hour a month. Our idea was that if we could get people more connected to how their food gets onto their table, they would see the bigger picture and be more thoughtful in their buying decisions.

Our first manager and I drove to Los Angeles; bought a used refrigeration unit, shelves, counters and cash registers; and then brought them to Isla Vista and set them up. We ordered our first shipment of food and had 40 or 50 volunteers helping to stock the shelves when it arrived. We had one of the local artisans make a beautiful wooden sign for the front of our store, and we were ready to open.

Seeing people streaming into this little 1,400-square-foot store that was filled with the shelves and counters we'd assembled ourselves was one of the most thrilling moments of my life to that point. We had a vision to change the world, we'd put it into action and it was working!

That euphoria continued until one night a couple months after the store had opened. I was doing the books in the small office at the back of the store when I got a rude shock. I discovered that some of our volunteer cashiers had been stealing money from the till!

I was in disbelief. *How could they take money from themselves?* I thought. Of course, they didn't realize that by stealing money from the Co-op, they were raising food prices for themselves and for all the other members. They were just looking at their own short-term benefit.

That moment was a turning point for me, as a big piece of my puzzle fell into place. I realized that it doesn't matter how well designed the structures of our social institutions are: if the people who are part of them aren't aware of the broader impact of their decisions, those institutions won't create real change.

Having put that part of the puzzle together, I shifted my focus. Several years earlier I'd learned the Transcendental Meditation (TM) technique, brought to the West by His Holiness Maharishi Mahesh Yogi. TM had been a huge help to me in dealing with the pressure of taking on big responsibilities at a young age, but, until this point, I had viewed it simply as a tool to relieve stress and allow me to do what really mattered.

Now, another piece of the puzzle fell into place: I realized that if I wanted to live in an enlightened world, I'd better start with myself. I became a teacher of TM and then, for more than 10 years, participated in a special program that had me meditating for 8 to 10 hours a day. During that time, I studied the Vedic literature of India extensively and began to gain an understanding of the fundamental structure of life.

By 1991, when I decided to return to the world, I thought I'd figured out the puzzle of my life. I was happy and excited to reenter an active life.

Then I got married and found myself in a tailspin for five long years. Without realizing it, I was being driven by the mistaken belief that I had to take work based on how much money the job paid. I had to be responsible. I had to support my wife and myself. So, for the first time in my life, I thought only of the salary, instead of whether I loved the work.

I went through one job after another, always looking for more money. And we went deeper and deeper into debt. When we were on the verge of bankruptcy, my wife suggested I try a different kind of job. This one didn't have a fancy title, and I'd only make a lot of money if I performed well. It felt kind of scary, but nothing was working, so I decided to try it.

It turned out that the skills and talents required for this new job—selling consulting and training services to Fortune 500 companies—were just those that I have. So I did well. I became one of my company's top producers and starting making more money than I had before in jobs with impressive titles.

Another puzzle piece dropped into place: success comes when you're using your learned skills and natural talents to provide value that others want.

I loved my new success for about 18 months. Then it began to feel like I was spinning my wheels. The excitement and challenge of learning a new job was replaced by the repetitiveness that came with having mastered it. I was suddenly forced to ask myself, *Do I love this work?* The answer was no.

Another piece of the puzzle fell into place: Using your skills and talents isn't enough. To be fulfilled in work and life, you must have a passion for what you're doing.

It was at this time that my now-ex-wife, Janet, thought to introduce me to her creation, "The Passion Test," a simple process for discovering what really matters to you. She'd only shared it with a handful of people by this point. She took me through it, and almost immediately my life began to change.

I began to consciously choose to do things that aligned me with my passions. Life started being fun again.

In my years of long meditation, I'd been introduced to the ancient Vedic science of timing called Jyotish. I'd seen the power of Jyotish several years earlier when a Jyotish consultant had told Janet she had to go visit her mother immediately. Janet followed this advice, had a wonderful visit with her mother and then, a few weeks later, her mother passed away unexpectedly.

I'd been thinking I would need to stay in my current job for at least a year to pay off my debts, despite feeling like I was spinning my wheels. Then I'd go back to the long-meditation program I'd loved so much.

I had a consultation with a Jyotish consultant, and it became clear that I needed to go back to that meditation program sooner or I'd likely never make it back. But I knew there were a few things that I had to take care of first in order to feel good about making that change:

- I'd been managing some property for my mother that was up for sale. If I just left, it wouldn't be fair to her, so her property had to sell before I could leave.
- I was a top performer at my company, and the company had treated me really well. So I didn't feel I could leave unless I found someone equally good to take my place.
- I still had loans to pay off, so I needed to have some form of income even while meditating most of the day.

I decided that if this was the right time for me to return to extended meditation, these three items would have to be fulfilled first.

Within a week, my mother received and accepted a purchase offer for her property. Within a month, one of my old buddies who'd been a top performer at another company was hired to take my place. Just before I was to leave, my company and I worked out a plan that would allow me to work for them a few hours each week, helping me pay off my debts.

Another puzzle piece fell into place that eventually ended up in the book we would write about The Passion Test: when you're clear, what you want will show up in your life, and only to the extent you're clear.

I went back to meditating 8 to 10 hours a day for the next year and was in heaven. But once again I was drawn to return to the world of activity when Janet asked me for a favor. A woman named Byron Katie had asked Janet to become her marketing director. Katie was a remarkable woman who taught a simple method for investigating one's beliefs, Janet said and asked me to come to her weekend workshop to decide if she should accept Katie's offer.

That weekend blew my mind. What was most remarkable was that as I applied the simple process of self-inquiry that Byron Katie calls "The Work," my whole experience shifted. I began to feel freer and more at ease than I ever had before.

Katie says that The Work is like a virus; once you start self-inquiry, it gains a life of its own. My mind began questioning everything, and, as thoughts that had been with me since childhood began to dissolve, life became more and more fun.

Over the next decade, Janet and I wrote *The Passion Test* and then *Your Hidden Riches*. We built a global brand with more than 1,500 facilitators in over 60 countries. I remarried in 2006 and we had three amazing children. My life was filled with love and rich in every way.

Then, in 2013, as we were looking for a school for our oldest daughter, a vision began to form in my mind. It started as a design for our ideal home and then, little by little, expanded into a vision that fulfills what my heart has longed for since that day when I watched the Bank of America burn to the ground.

That vision goes by the name of the Beyul Club & Resorts. The Club's mission and purpose is to support each Member in "solving the puzzle of their own life," while, at the same time, helping them realize their personal passion projects. The Club's ultimate aim is to create a model of a new way of living, a model of how heaven can be lived on earth.

The Club will provide knowledge, tools and relationships that allow each Member to solve their own life's puzzle. Members will know when the pieces of their life fall into place as they experience deep peace, a profound sense of purpose and a growing level of fulfillment.

The Club will offer its Members the opportunity to learn from and interact with world-renowned mentors and trainers in the areas of personal growth and fulfillment, business skills, relationships and family, health and more.

The Club will be anchored by unique, luxurious retreats, the first of which is planned for the beautiful coastline of Costa Rica, where Members can bring their families, learn from high-profile mentors and trainers, network and participate in special events.

These resorts will use both ancient wisdom and modern methods of architecture to create an environment unlike any other—one that is simultaneously beautiful, deeply peaceful and designed holistically to be completely sustainable. The community that Members will enjoy while at the physical Beyul Resorts will be sustained by an online community of Members.

I'm lit up by this vision. But it's a $100-million project. I've created a detailed plan and financial projections and gathered support from colleagues, and yet I find myself forced to be comfortable living in what Byron Katie calls the "don't-know mind."

And with this experience, another puzzle piece drops into place: not knowing what will happen or how it will happen, and being comfortable in not knowing, makes life so exciting. There's no telling what will come next. Everything that shows up is fresh and unexpected. Life becomes truly remarkable.

As you put the pieces of your own puzzle together, remember that you're not alone. Choose to connect with others, learn from others, support others and work with others. Because another glorious piece of this puzzle of life is the power of a team. And, as my children will tell you, T-E-A-M stands for "Together Everyone Achieves Miracles."

Chris Attwood is co-author of the New York Times *bestsellers* The Passion Test *and* Your Hidden Riches. *He is also president and founder of the Beyul Club & Resorts (www.beyulclub.com). Chris lives with his wife, Doris, and his three children, Sophie, Tianna and Chetan in Iowa, Germany and Costa Rica.*

Chapter 4

Honor the Call!

Alison Braithwaite

Have you ever had the feeling that the universe was conspiring *for* you? Maybe nudging you in a certain direction or even calling you to action? I had that feeling at a critical point in my life, and following it was one of the best things I ever did. It changed my whole approach to life.

I had a job as an environmental manager, and it was meaningful work, but I wasn't enjoying it. In fact, I was toughing it out day by day, feeling frustrated, like there was something more I was supposed to be doing. And then, one day, that feeling—that call to action—came up out of the blue, and even though I brushed it aside a few times, it didn't go away. After a couple of weeks, it was still there and it was crystal clear.

I should go to Costa Rica and learn Spanish.

Really? I thought.

Why?

I didn't know anyone in Costa Rica…or even anyone who spoke Spanish. But the feeling didn't go away. It was pulling me like a magnet and growing in strength until I realized it could not be ignored. I had to follow it to see where it would lead me.

Looking back, I call this one of the pivotal moments in my life when I "honored the call." Whenever I honor the call, my life blossoms, I embrace discovery and I feel fulfilled. Let me tell you the story of how it happened, and as I share this story, I'll also tell you the five lessons I learned that can support you in honoring your call and living a more enlightened life.

Lesson #1: Listen, Consider and Take Action

When I say I felt I had to go to Costa Rica and learn Spanish, I knew that would mean going to live there for at least a few months and maybe longer. So, it was a pretty radical step for me, involving giving up my job and more, and I had to seriously think about it. *Was it a smart idea? Did it make sense in my life?*

Well, I wasn't exactly excited about my current job—and I had always wanted to live in another country and learn another language—so why *not* take the plunge and travel to Costa Rica?

I quit my job, giving a significant amount of notice, and when time passed and they saw that I was serious about leaving, they offered me a leave of absence for eight months. I cheered inside: *the universe is on my side!* So, I took action, honored the call and left for Costa Rica.

This is the first step to a more enlightened life: you must listen to what's calling you and act upon it. It's calling you for a reason. If you let the call fade away, it's a missed opportunity. You must find a way to step toward your calling and trust that the universe supports you.

And this isn't just about the big choices in life. This is true even if the call is something quite simple and everyday, like *I should turn right here rather than left* or *I should say something to that person over there.* Consider whether it's wise and if so, respond to the call! And notice what opens up for you.

Lesson #2: Be the Author of Your Own Life

Before I left, I wrote about what I wanted the experience to be but with a twist: I wrote as if I were writing about the past, as if I had already experienced the adventure that I was just launching into. This is actually an annual ritual for me. At the end of each year, I write about the year coming up as if I'm looking back on it. Doing this, I've found that words have amazing power. The written word feels like a magic wand that helps me create what I want.

Writing about what's to come also heightens my sense of adventure and opens my mind to the opportunities that lie ahead. Writing can act as a guidepost, something to check back with as I ask myself, *Am I still aligned with my vision?* When I wrote about my experience in Costa Rica, I described being part of a community and learning Spanish easily with a close friend. I wrote about being active outdoors and enjoying the beauty of nature. It gave me thrills of happiness to imagine it all.

Try it now! Take some time to write your vision for your future. Unleash your imagination without judging what comes out—just allow the words to flow. What is it you want to experience? What do you want to learn—and feel? Take the time to write it down, and try writing it as if it has already happened, as if your future self is writing a diary entry.

Several years after my time in Costa Rica, I came across a journal that described my experience there. As I read it, I thought, *Well, that's not quite right. It's close but not quite right.* Then I realized that I was reading what I had written prior to going there! I was stunned to see how closely it was aligned with my actual experiences.

Lesson #3: Let Go of Judgment and Embrace Trust

I always feel a sense of flow when I'm traveling. I trust that I'm being looked after, and I'm open to exploring, learning and connecting. So, I headed to Costa Rica feeling open to the possibilities. My first intention was to learn Spanish, so I signed up to go to a Spanish school in the capital city, San José. This wasn't aligned with my vision of learning with a friend, but I didn't trust my vision yet, and I felt I had to somehow address my fear of landing in a new country, unable to communicate.

That decision resulted in a couple of miserable weeks in San José. Everything was frustrating and exhausting for me there. So, I checked back in with my inner vision and felt a call to move to Monteverde, the Green Mountain. A region high in the famed "cloud forest" of Costa Rica, it seemed likely to suit my love of nature better.

As I traveled there in a small van, it was a long, slow climb up a rocky dirt road with a spectacular view the whole way. At the top, I stepped out into Monteverde and rejoiced. Now, *this* was my place! It was alive with green. I could see and feel the texture of green and smell the fragrance of green. I could even *hear* green as the leaves rustled in the wind.

In the coming days, I felt at home, surrounded by the cloud forest, walking wherever I needed to go. This is what had called me, this was what my soul had hungered to experience and this was where I would stay for a while.

After two miserable weeks in a language school in Monteverde, something had to change. I love school, but, for me, learning a language in a school environment is painful. Fortunately, as I was considering my options, I came upon a flyer offering art classes with local artists. My heart leapt up: I had always wanted to study art! I felt something precious had been offered to me, so I called the number on the flyer. Soon I was being driven out to meet one of the artists, passing through rolling, green vistas.

We arrived at a charming house with a stone path to the door. As I climbed out of the car, a lovely woman came out of the house and greeted us. I immediately recognized her as the friend I was looking for. Ana is a gentle soul with vibrant eyes and a loving smile who opens her heart and her home to everyone.

Ana led us into her studio, a spacious room so full of light it was hard to tell where the inside ended and the outside began. It was the perfect expression of Ana. On the easel in the center of the room was a partly finished painting of vibrant blues and greens, and the rest of the studio was full of magical pottery creations, including images of women appearing as trees and other forms of nature that drew me in powerfully. I loved the themes of Ana's art, and I instantly wanted to learn how to work with clay. I totally trusted that this was the place for me, and this was the friend I could learn from.

Trusting your positive feelings opens you up to opportunities. Notice how open and expanded you feel when you trust? Trusting allows your life to unfold. It keeps you aligned with the call, even when things aren't going exactly the way you had dreamed.

If we get stuck in judgment or fear or doubt, we close ourselves down. If those emotions do appear, just notice them and move through them. Don't indulge in them. Instead, shift your feelings by indulging in something that makes you feel expansive, like dance, meditation, art, song, nature or being with family and loved ones. Indulge in what you love, remain open for the next discovery and trust that you will know the next step when you see it.

Lesson #4: See Yourself as Capable and Be with Others Who Do Too

Ana accepted me as her student, even though I told her I had never worked with clay before and my art experience was limited to drawing stick people. The first day we met for class, she handed me a piece of paper and told me to draw what I would like to create with the clay. My first reaction was internal panic. *I don't know how to draw! What if I can't do this?* But Ana saw me as being capable, so I let go of my judgment and decided I was capable, as well.

Sure enough, I liked what I drew and I was surprised by what I could create right away. Making art took me to a space of timelessness where my senses took over and my mind was trusting. I felt freedom and ease as I began to create forms from clay. It was like the clay guided me to create something already manifested on some level.

Learning Spanish became easy, too. Ana and I gradually began to speak more and more in Spanish, just as friends, which removed the judgment and pressure to perform that school had brought. Working together, we had the ease of conversation that comes when you're both in a place of caring and curiosity.

Why not try it now in your life? See yourself and others as capable and surround yourself with people who see you as capable. That first day with Ana, when we both did this, somehow it allowed my creativity to flow. I surprised myself—and I delighted myself. Since then, I've come to think that we underestimate ourselves and others far too often.

Gandhi once said, "The difference between what we do and what we are capable of would suffice to solve most of the world's problems." So, if there is something that you would like to do, see yourself as capable and do it. And, in the same way, imagine what the person you want to be would be like—and you will grow steadily in that direction and one day be there.

Lesson #5: Allow the Flow to Happen

After I had spent a week as Ana's student, the pieces I was creating were of a quality that they could be sold, and Ana asked me to stay on and create art with her. Each day, as I walked from my pensión to Ana's home along the dirt roads of the green mountain, I felt an aliveness that made me feel like anything was possible. I had found community with Ana and the expatriates on the mountain, and I had also found a spiritual practice, sitting in a circle in silence each Sunday in a very simple Quaker meetinghouse. Our community continually opened up opportunities for me to experience things and learn lessons that I needed to learn. I felt a sense of belonging, a sense of acceptance. I spent much of my day surrounded by nature, and I had powerful conversations about things that really mattered.

Yet another door opened when I signed up for a dance class. Dance was something I had done as a young child and then stopped. As an adult, I had told myself I couldn't dance, but now I wanted to try it again. In class I let go into the flow of the music and the struggle was gone.

Dance created even more flow in my life. One afternoon, I was walking to class thinking that it would be so nice to go to the beach, which I still hadn't done. I imagined the sand under my feet and the warm sun on my skin. Moments later, when I got to my dance class, a woman announced that she was heading to the beach for the weekend after class, and we were all welcome to join her. The synchronicity was magical! I went to the beach, and I danced on the sand.

Those days profoundly changed my perspective and approach to life. When I returned to home, I ended up back at my former company as director of environmental performance. As a result of my experiences in Costa Rica, I went from resenting my work to loving the chance to create an environmental program that engaged and empowered employees in making a difference by seeing themselves as the environment in their work and their lives.

When you let go of judgment and start trusting, your life begins to flow. At first you might doubt it, but let your intuition guide you and you'll start noticing the flow. Try taking a day, or an hour, just to meander. Start in the place that you feel you want to start, and move in the direction that you feel you want to move.

Move from a place of trust, like you know your own path. Notice what's around you, and when something piques your curiosity or calls you for a closer look, move toward it. Notice what shows up.

In the 1700s, the German philosopher Immanuel Kant defined "enlightenment" as the state of having the courage and decisiveness to follow your own wisdom without the guidance of another. Notice your wisdom and let it guide you. Act upon it and then celebrate the results. The more you acknowledge and celebrate your moments of enlightenment, the more life flows.

Imagine what the world would be like if we all lived from the place where the universe conspires with us, a place of trust, nonjudgment, expansion and ease. Imagine how different the world would be if we all created from that place. The world is crying out for each one of us to recognize our own magnificence and step into the full expression of ourselves. What's calling you? And what's your first step in that direction? Honor the call and take that step!

A nature-centered leadership coach, facilitator and speaker, Alison Braithwaite inspires professional women to let go of their "supposed-tos" and grow to fully express themselves. She is the author of Letting Go of "Supposed To": Five Steps to Live Your Nature, *a collection of interviews with female leaders who are taking action on their dreams for the world. Their stories inspired Alison to use nature as a model to thrive. Nature is resilient, creative, interconnected, cyclical and whole. Alison believes that nature has within itself all that it needs to fully express its potential, just as every individual and organization does.*

With 25 years of experience in leadership roles in the environmental sector, Alison is uniquely placed to facilitate a transformative and self-reflective process that involves nature, art and strategic-visioning exercises. Alison holds a master's in leadership and a graduate certificate in executive coaching from Royal Roads University. Visit her at alisonbraithwaite.com.

Chapter 5

This Is It! This is Life:
Three Tips for Living It Fully
Lori Woodley

Everything changed the day I turned 25. My father had suddenly fallen ill, and the whole family was gathered in his hospital room to hear the diagnosis. When the doctor pointed out the brain tumor on the backlit X-ray board, my world cracked. When we were told the tumor was aggressive and treatment would only be a temporary Band-Aid, my world collapsed. My marathon-running father—a trusted friend to all, a brilliant engineer and my 49-year-old personal hero—was going to die.

My dad was his steady self. "I'm not going anywhere," he said. "I promise you I'll live to bounce a grandchild on my knee."

Married just two months prior, my husband and I weren't planning to have children for some time. However, that plan went out the window when we heard Dad's words—even though that wasn't entirely sensible. Both of us were in master's programs and there were no spare minutes or dollars for a child, or for a father who was terminally ill.

32

Nonetheless, in the coming days and weeks, doctors and hospitals became a huge part of our world, along with full-time jobs, night classes and financial difficulties. It was a challenging time, but my dad was brave, our rock, as always. We all kept it together, one moment to the next—what else was there to do?

And three months later I victoriously added pregnancy to my list of current projects. I felt joy about my coming baby, yet it was juxtaposed with grief over my dad's condition. These strong, conflicting emotions had both my mind and heart spinning, leaving me feeling a kind of simmering numbness.

The next nine months were intense for us all. I remember being seven months pregnant and holding my dad's hand as the doctor pulled the respirator from his lungs, knowing that he would likely not be able to breathe on his own. Thank God, he did, his determination and strength showing up once again. This hospitalization had come just days following his 50th birthday party, which he celebrated at home with an overflow of people who loved and admired him. At that time, his non-contagious pneumonia was really bad; the doctors were amazed he survived it. Bouncing his grandchild was his goal, and he had two months to go.

During those long, sometimes torturous months, I was also experiencing human greatness and love at a depth I had never felt before. Prior to that, I had always thought, *I've got this! If it's to be, it's up to me.* But that challenge showed me that I, and all of us, can't do it as well on our own. People showed up throughout my dad's illness to help, support or simply ease the process in whatever way they could. These were actions I was used to doing as a giver; it was new territory to be a receiver. Again my conflicting emotions were wrestling with each other. I was living in a world I often felt could not possibly be real.

My joy and sorrow had the ultimate face-off two months later, when our baby girl arrived, the very same day my dad came home to live his last days with us. We gathered in the living room around his hospital bed, and he held his first and only grandchild, just eight hours old.

It was clear to us all that Dad felt complete now and was ready to move out of the physical world of pain and into whatever was next for him. Eleven days after our daughter was born, a group of Dad's closest friends and colleagues circled around him and read *Oh the Places You'll Go!* by Dr. Seuss. Tearful and deeply touched, they said their good-byes. Later that night, my dad took his final earthly breath with my mom, sister, brother, husband and me, holding his new granddaughter, close beside him.

Tears rolled down my face and the lyric "Be at peace," from *Les Misérables's* "Come to Me," sang in my head. I stood there beside him, holding my newborn child, torn in two. The worst and the best were happening at the exact same time, and I felt deeply conflicted. How does one make sense of this and move forward from it? How does one embrace it all authentically and not "stuff" one extreme feeling or the other?

Part of me felt it would be reasonable to feel "poor me" feelings at the unfairness of my father's early death, along with my grief. On the other hand, it would be so easy to bury myself in my daughter as a savior from the pain. But how unfair would that be to her? Of course, she was a comfort to me, but I believe children should be able to come into the world without the obligation to "fix" broken parts of the adults in their lives. It is not a child's responsibility to do this. Finding my joy was my own responsibility. Wasn't it?

My emotional confusion was coming like a wildfire; the answers, like molasses. Unwittingly, I settled into a state of numbness (what I now refer to as my slow fade into oblivion), trusting that my emotional turmoil would ease up over time. Next year would be better. I kept waiting for it to get better. Someday, out there in the future, it would get better.

And then, it didn't.

Over the next few years, I had my son—my second most joyful life-moment—and at the same time I also attended an unreasonable number of funerals. Seven were for close family members and friends, three of whom I was with as they took their last breaths. One year we lost all three remaining members of my dad's side of the family. Also, financially, life was really challenging for my husband and me. I had to go back to work just two weeks after my son was born, and for a while we were living with my mom and sleeping in my childhood room.

All along I continued to take an inventory of my feelings, mostly discovering that I wasn't always feeling. A lot of the time, I simply existed.

I was moving from event to event, not fully present, but still presenting the world with an "I've got this and you are awesome!" smile. I was getting life done and being everyone's everything, all while feeling anesthetized. Drugged, but not.

And then came the epiphany, which I imagined as the sound of the space shuttle reentering the atmosphere. It happened as I heard a friend say, "I can't wait for the New Year! It has to get better!"

A visceral awakening shot through me, and I wanted to shake her and yell, "Don't wait! Don't wait! You'll miss all the good stuff along the way, and you'll be constantly disappointed because it doesn't *get* better! It's *already* better! It's LIFE! It's all just *Life.*"

From that moment on, my numbness began to fade, and I started living more fully in the present moment, feeling whatever feelings were there, mixed together or on their own. This waking up to life as it is *now* became a way of being for me. Of course, I had to learn how to deal with the various feelings that came up, and I was, and am, far from perfect at it. I still have to give myself permission to feel my feelings at times.

But I've learned one thing for sure: Yes, the feelings that come up in each moment can sometimes be painful to experience. But the honesty and inspired growth that come from living openly through all emotions is so powerful that life is always better on the other side. *Always.*

The gift of feeling your feelings, even when they're conflicting or painful, is profound peace and freedom. And, also, liberation from judgment and victimization! To find this peace and liberation within you, I offer the following three principles, and the Live-It Tips that come with each.

Principle #1: Life Events Aren't Personal

When it comes to Mother Nature and all her beautiful and beastly aspects, there seems to be no way to make rhyme or reason of events. Man-made climate change aside, Mother Nature rains and storms when she wants to and shines bright and warm when she wants to. She's not, however, doing this "to us"; she's simply doing it. And through these doings, she's also sprouting new growth, feeding nations, cleansing the air we breathe and providing varying degrees of health to all. She does this neutrally.

On the other hand, we humans often make events personal; we feel they're being done "to us." For instance, when someone makes a choice that hurts us we say, "They did X to me." This is powerless and defeated thinking. In reality, they didn't do anything "to you"; they simply did something. Your reaction is up to you. And you can do something helpful or harmful to yourself with your reaction.

By embracing the fact that nothing is being done to us, we claim powerful ownership of our lives rather than victimization. We accept circumstances as they are and, from that peaceful place, can work toward improving them. On the other hand, when we speak of what "should be," we're powerless because we're not living in the reality of here and now.

You can put these concepts into practice with the following...

Live-It Tips:
- *Notice* the times when you think or say things that come from a sense of being wronged by life, including the actions of others. Notice how powerless and victimized this makes you feel.
- *Choose* to see life from the perspective of neutrality: "This is just happening; no one's out to get me." See a challenge as just that, a challenge, not a sign that life is purposely attacking you.
- **Act** in ways that hold you high and powerful. Say "it happened," instead of "he did it." Say "I feel hurt," instead of "you hurt me." Embrace the reality that life is both joyous and painful, sometimes at the same time. Assign no blame to what is happening; just be with it.

Principle #2: Be Responsible for Your Feelings

Once we stop being victims, the next step is to own our feelings. This can be a bit scary because taking ownership seems more difficult than pointing fingers. But we don't fully live if we don't own our "stuff"! We just continue to be victims, and there's no power, peace or joy in that way of living.

When we act from the perspective that nothing was done "to us," we can embrace what we're experiencing and how we're responding. When someone harms us or fires us or steals from us, we can come from the old paradigm of "they ruined my life," or from a new paradigm of "this is hard, this feels bad and life is changing." We can still be scared, sad and angry; we just need to embrace those feelings, go through them, process them as ours and be sure we're not spreading them to others.

We're hurting ourselves if we're feeling self-pity or blaming others. We only have an opportunity to thrive when we own our feelings, and that sounds like "this happened, and I feel bad, and I'm going to do X to make myself feel better." That is self-empowerment, which in turn brings confidence and freedom.

Live-It Tips:
- *Notice* your feelings. Do you own them as yours? Or are you making them someone else's fault? Are you snapping at your family or at the grocery store clerk? Are you telling everyone you know the story of "what happened to you," hoping for sympathy and validation?
- *Choose* to *actually feel* your feelings, without minimizing or denying them. When you feel them, they will move and eventually leave. Feel them, name them and move through them, regardless of how challenging that is—and don't drag others into it. Choose the belief that "the only way out is through."
- *Act* in ways that hold you accountable for your feelings and your actions based on those feelings. Speak of them honestly. And do all you can to allow others to stay happy even when you are not, even if it means excusing yourself for a cooling-off walk or drive.

Principle #3: Look for the Upside and Focus on It

Even in the most challenging times, we can choose to do something that will improve the quality of our own life and others' lives—or not. It can be hard when we're in pain, maybe feeling a loss, to decide to lean toward what is good in this moment, instead of bemoaning "what's happening to me." Yet, when we seek to find the upside, or the lessons learned, we gain an understanding that offsets our pain and brings a sense of purpose. A sense of purpose is a blessing when we're suffering.

Today, I can even find upsides in the heartbreaking loss of my dad. The reality is that my daughter wouldn't have been born if my dad hadn't become ill. And I might not have had such a powerful wake-up call, one that changed every day of my life since then for the better. I know Dad would be so happy about that.

Live-It Tips:
- *Notice*, in the midst of an upset: are you focused on what's wrong with this situation and who's to blame for it? Or are you feeling your feelings and looking for the value of this moment, hard as it might be to find at first?
- *Choose* to look for the gifts and opportunities that can come out of hard events. Choose to purposefully redirect your thoughts as many times as it takes to see the good that's there, so you can rebound from hardship faster and renew your own life sooner.
- *Act* in ways that drive you to find new purpose and direction in each challenge. Engage in conversations about your appreciation of things, rather than your victimization. Let others know you're looking for the upside, and allow them to contribute theirs. Seek professional help if, over time, you can't make peace with a particular event and find yourself wading neck-deep in the "wrong" that happened to you.

When we wake up and live these principles, we stop waiting for life to get better and start living fully in the victories and challenges of the present. We embrace our whole life, and that lets us thrive beyond our wildest imaginations.

Whenever I think of my dad now, I thank him. For being a wonderful dad and a beautiful man. For touching the lives of so many with his love. For showing me how to live a great life, both in his living and in his dying. Always now, deep in my heart, I see his beloved smile and I feel his peace.

Notice Choose Act®

Public speaker, trainer and author in communication, social impact and public service, Lori is co-founder and executive director for All It Takes, a nonprofit organization that teaches bold and compassionate leadership.

After earning her master's degree in educational psychology, Lori spent 25 years in school counseling. Through those years, she also navigated the varied complexities of the entertainment industry as interest in her daughter Shailene Woodley's talent rose. Walking the walk, Lori is a role model for social justice activism, and most recently became involved in the Standing Rock Sioux Tribe fight against the Dakota Access Pipeline.

As a counselor, Lori recognizes the compelling need for youth to actively engage in purposeful thought followed by action in order to reduce risk factors, including bullying, drug use and suicide. Lori's programs target how youth see themselves, such that they become individual and collective change agents, purpose-driven catalysts for social climate change.

Chapter 6

Step by Step to Stillness:
A Busy Person's Guide to Peak Results
Guillermo Paz

T his chapter is for high-energy, nonstop entrepreneurial types of people who want to cut straight to the bottom line. If you're the kind of person who skips the instructions when assembling something because it's faster for you to figure it out yourself, this chapter is for you.

This approach is typical for business people because we're trained to always be looking for the "Next," rather than focusing on the "Now." We get our sales reports or our client statements and immediately start planning our next sale or looking for our next client. But what we don't realize is this: if we stop and experience the Now on a regular basis, we'll soon find we're *attracting* the Next.

Why? Because experiencing the Now is like splitting the atom: it releases the greatest force of energy in the universe. So stepping into the Now is the most powerful tool we possess to attract whatever we want.

And being grounded in the stillness of the Now, even in the midst of activity, is essential if you want to do the following:

- Quiet the "mind chatter" and distractions to focus on your most important work
- Connect to a flow of new ideas and opportunities
- Improve your health by relieving stress and boosting the immune system
- Understand your purpose of being and get into a state of higher awareness

I like this spiritually charged expression: "When you're quiet, you can hear the whisper of your soul." From a business perspective, I translate it as "When you're quiet and connected to Source, you open to an inflow of new ideas, energy and inspirations for your next decision."

This means your workday really begins when you access the power source that will fuel your day and generate inspiration. How? By taking the time to experience stillness. And that's easy. Let me show you how.

How to Begin

When I talk to people, particularly fellow business people, about the benefits of meditation, or practicing stillness, many say, "I can't do that. My mind is too active. There's no way I can control the chatter." Or "I don't have the time to meditate." And I understand. That's life for some people, and I can't argue with life.

But if that's your situation, I say, practice stillness as soon as you wake up, just for five or 10 minutes before getting out of bed. As you may have heard, it's better to practice stillness while sitting down with the spine erect, so sit up in bed if you can. But, in any case, it's better to do it while still in bed for just five to 10 minutes, than not at all.

And if you haven't figured out how to take five or 10 minutes for yourself out of the 1,440 minutes there are in a day, I say, "Friend, you don't have a life. It's time to get one!"

Meeting Stillness

We meet stillness the moment we make a conscious decision to stop thinking about the past or the future. There are lots of ways to train the mind to do that—I suggest you try one that has worked great for me. It's a matter of training, like the training you do in a gym. You don't go in the first day and expect to pump four 50-pound plates. You gradually grow into it. But, trust me, *everyone* can do it.

Many modalities to control the mind are available online and on YouTube, but I encourage you to try the one I outline below. It's easy and it doesn't even require an Internet connection. Give it a try and I think you'll be hooked.

Still the Mind 101: Control the Chatter

First, with your eyes closed, be aware of your whole body and also be aware of any uncomfortable areas in your body. Take a deep breath, exhale slowly and mentally say, *I'm relaxing my body.* This first step is really that simple. Do this about five times or until you feel the tension has left your body.

With the body relaxed, move on to relaxing the mind. To still your mind (which, if it's anything like mine, runs like a horse stampede), you have to distract it with another thought or another task. Try this:

Be aware of the air touching the tip of your nose as you inhale and exhale slowly, as follows:

Count to six while inhaling.
Hold the breath for three counts.
Exhale for six counts.
Hold the breath for three counts.
Repeat.

This is called pranic (pronounced "prah' nic") breathing, as defined by Master Choa Kok Sui, founder of the modern Pranic Healing method. It's the first step to stilling the mind. Focusing on the air touching the tip of your nose is essential because it takes your mind away from thoughts of past or future events. If thoughts keep coming, just easily come back to focusing on the tip of your nose. The goal here is to stop thinking of past or future events, and be present.

Do this breathing cycle 10 times, always focusing on the tip of your nose. You will feel your shoulders drop, your belly expand, your arms and thighs relax, and you might even feel your heart rate slowing down. You are giving your mind and body a break. Remember that the goal here is to quiet the mind, more than the breathing. You can practice this early every morning, during your workday, at a religious service, while waiting in line or any other time you feel you want to relax or experiment with living a more connected life.

Note that, once you've practiced for several days, you won't need to count anymore to get the right pace of breathing. It will be automatic.

Now, before you move on to Stillness 202, stop reading and practice 101 for a few minutes.

Still the Mind 202: A Shortcut to Stillness

There's a simple trick, or shortcut, to creating stillness that scientists have found, and also a technical explanation of why it works, based on the frequency of our brain waves. The following simple action "forces" your brain into an alpha state at any time of day: close your eyes, and, while taking a deep breath in, roll your eyes upward. Then, while exhaling, bring your eyes back to their normal position. You just need to do that once, not continuously.

Try it now, gently, and see if you notice a subtle quieting of the mind. This happens because the brain reacts to the upward eye roll by generating alpha waves. Have you ever noticed that you automatically roll your eyes upward when you're trying to remember something? The body does that because it triggers the production of alpha waves in the brain, which provide a bridge to the subconscious mind and also take your mind to a state of greater stillness.

When you're fully awake, your brain-wave frequency is around 20 Hz (cycles per second), which is in the beta spectrum. When you're waking up in the morning, right at the moment between sleeping and waking, your brain-wave frequency is at 10 cycles per second, which is in the alpha spectrum. And when you still your mind or meditate, and even sometimes while praying, you also bring your brain waves down to the quieter alpha wavelength.

It just so happens that our planet pulses at around 8 Hz, which is also in the alpha spectrum. That means that, when you're in an alpha state, you're in harmony with our planet's own vibratory wavelength. We all know how well things go in our personal and professional life when we're in harmony with those we engage with. This is like that but on a more profound level.

After you do the eye roll described above, you'll find it's easier to focus on the air at the tip of the nose and do the breathing exercise. Try it now, and continue with the breathing for a few minutes before you go on to Stillness 303.

Still the Mind 303: To Go Deeper, Add a "Connecting" Word

When you feel you're starting to still your mind with the steps covered so far, you can add another layer to go deeper into stillness, as follows:

Choose a word that makes you feel expanded or connected to the universe or the Divine, and say it silently while doing the pranic breathing. Some people use the word "love" or "amen" or "om," but you can use any one- or two-syllable word that will help you connect in a spiritual or unifying way. Some pointers:

- When using a two-syllable word, say the first syllable during the inhalation and the second during the exhalation.
- When using words with "m" or "n" sounds, such as "amen" or "om," note that these sounds create the most internal vibration, so linger on them and visualize every cell in your body resonating with them.
- When using a single-syllable word, such as "om" or "love," say it once during the inhalation and again throughout the exhalation.

A note on the word "om": it's often perceived as belonging to the Eastern philosophies, but it's actually a universal sound. It's part of the prefix "omni-," which means "all" and is used to express qualities of God, such as omnipotence, omniscience and omnipresence.

If you've taken the subway in London, you're familiar with the sign "Mind the Gap." In this practice we're going to do the same. The moment of silence, or the gap, between inhalation and exhalation is a "transcendent moment" that we want to be aware of. Be alert to it and to the depth of stillness there, and be receptive to the energy moving through your body and the vibration of all your cells in harmony at that time.

Before we move on, take a few minutes to practice Stillness 303. Let's review the steps:

1. With eyes closed, breathe deeply a few times while mentally saying, *I'm relaxing my body.*
2. Roll the eyes up once to access the alpha state.
3. Put your attention on the air at the tip of your nose, and do pranic breathing.
4. Easily begin repeating your connecting word.
5. Continue with the practice for five or 10 minutes, or as long as you like.

This may seem like a lot at first, but, with daily practice, it soon becomes almost effortless. Just let your awareness be on each of the different elements in a very easy, unforced way. Straining or trying is counterproductive.

Still the Mind 404: You Don't Travel the Inner World Alone

Now that the inner door is opening for you, I want to share the experience I have upon getting there. So far, we've been talking about practicing stillness just as a tool for achieving greater productivity, but for me and many others there's another dimension to it: it can lead you naturally to an awareness of something bigger than yourself. What I experience is a realization that I'm not alone. When I say the names of my spiritual teachers before practicing stillness, their spiritual energy is with me in that journey.

Even if you're not a person who ever prays, check it out. If you invoke the name of Jesus or Krishna or Allah or any other spiritual teacher or form of the Divine, or Higher Power or Source, my experience is that those you name do accompany you on the journey. Call on them when traveling in the nonphysical world, the energy world, and you'll never be alone.

If this idea strikes a chord, take a moment to invoke whomever you choose before beginning your meditation, and, if you want to, ask for their guidance, protection and illumination in that journey of discovery. And then, don't expect anything, but just be open to an evolutionary expansion of your being.

To track your experiences and the changes that occur, keep a journal and record significant moments. And, on a practical level, think of how much stress you have on a scale of 1 to 10 before practicing stillness, and write down that number. Then, afterwards, do another self-evaluation to see if the number went down, and keep track of that number, too.

Benefits of Stillness

The concept of stillness can be found in the earliest spiritual writings and teachings, from the Bible to all the Eastern philosophies. "Be still and know that I am God" is a famous and well-loved passage from Psalms in the Bible. All other religious teachings and many modern self-help techniques, including energy-healing modalities and yoga, have stillness at their core. It's the common denominator, the gateway to our spiritual realm, a state above and beyond our physical self. Think of it this way: when you pray, you talk; when you practice stillness, you listen.

There are also practical benefits of stillness, which are different for different people. Some value learning how to stop the mind's chatter so they can focus better on their work. Others welcome the flow of new ideas that can come after times of stillness. And some just enjoy the quiet time and the increased energy afterwards. One thing everyone appreciates is that their health improves when they reduce their stress levels by practicing stillness. Stillness also gives your immune system a break from the daily beating we tend to give it through our work, our eating habits, our strenuous mental exertions and the stress of everyday life.

A key takeaway is the understanding that action and stillness are equally important, and having a combination of both can upgrade your game. After practicing stillness, you may notice that you can think about your challenges more clearly, whether it's because they look smaller and less urgent or because you have shifted into a position of managing them, rather than reacting to them. The shift from living a reactive life to an active life is a big plus—for you and for everyone around you.

Once you're enjoying the practical benefits of practicing stillness, another by-product appears: you naturally move into a state of higher awareness of who you are and what you are connected to. On this level, I see stillness as a way to connect to my higher self, as well as to a higher power. This allows me to see my life as part of a bigger whole, rather than just existing in my immediate surroundings.

These days, once I relax physically, I can tap into my higher self pretty automatically. I get into a state of being an observer of myself, as if I were in a theater watching a play of Guillermo doing his daily chores or closing a deal. (An even deeper level is realizing that I don't *have* a soul, the soul has *me* in physical form—but that's a discussion for another chapter!) This simple but deep realization has helped me understand the famous phrase "You are not a drop of water in the ocean, but rather the entire ocean in a drop." When that truth hits, you realize you are one with God and one with all.

Now it's your turn. Take a few moments to check it out. The steps I've shared are simple… but so is stillness. See if it might up your game.

A successful entrepreneur, Guillermo Paz is now leveraging his lifelong process of self-discovery to launch a new spiritual venture: teaching people of all beliefs how to connect to their higher selves. To anyone frustrated by not being able to materialize their dreams, Guillermo says, "You must first become what you're asking for because you will not get what you want in life; you will get what you are. And the quickest way to transform yourself is by using your soul energy." To take the first step toward gaining mastery in this area, go to www.YourSoulDNA.com.

A "student of energy" from age 15, Guillermo has been practicing energy healing and Arhatic Yoga for the last 19 years at Master Choa Kok Sui's School of Pranic Healing. He spearheaded the launch of an annual meditation retreat in Puerto Rico and has also served as a mastermind facilitator at Jack Canfield's luxury retreats.

Remember
you are
Powerful Beyond
Measure!
love Cindy xo

— Chapter 7 —

Live Your Dream Life!
How Releasing Emotional Pain Heals the Body
Cynthia Mazzaferro

I jolted awake, startled and gasping for air! Panic ran through my whole body as it fought to survive. Finally, after five or 10 horror-filled seconds, my breathing pattern resumed and I fell back asleep, only to have the cycle repeat itself, again and again.

This had been going on for a while, and my husband, Tom, often lay awake in concern, wondering if his beloved wife was on her last breath. Worse, my chronic freight-train snoring often forced Tom out of our bed, which robbed us both of the intimacy we desired. I loved Tom very much, and it was breaking my heart that he was finding it harder and harder to sleep with me. I was embarrassed and hurt, even though I understood why he left. I felt deeply alone, despite having a loving husband and two wonderful sons.

My dream life was becoming a nightmare.

I finally mentioned these issues to my doctor and learned that I had a condition called sleep apnea, which kept me from getting enough oxygen. A sleep study was scheduled, and the results were scary: I only had a 50-percent sleep efficiency, no REM (deep restorative sleep) and 35 apnea-hypopnea events per hour. That's all bad news! Plus, I was 60 pounds overweight and had high blood pressure, so this was becoming a life-threatening situation.

"Good news!" they told me. There was a machine that would help me sleep normally. A few nights later, I put on the paraphernalia of what I called "the breathing machine" and thought, *This is worse.* Previously, I had felt bad about keeping my husband up at night—now I was mortified to even be seen. A mask covered my nose and was connected by a hose to a machine that generated a continuous flow of air pressure to keep my airway open. Very feminine and attractive… not in the least!

Once I was hooked up, it was awkward to snuggle—and forget about kissing. I found myself turning away from Tom, so he wouldn't see me like this. Yes, I was getting a better quality of sleep and feeling more rested, but my emotional well-being was deteriorating. I felt like a failure, and although Tom never said anything, I knew he was feeling the strain, too.

One night, fed up and frustrated, I tried something different. I went to bed quite late to let Tom get some undisturbed sleep, and then I tried to sleep without using the breathing machine. I placed pillows around me to try to keep myself from lying on my back, and I fell asleep. But it didn't work; I awoke many times, gasping for air and after a bit, I felt Tom get up and retreat to our spare bedroom.

In that moment, the memory of my father walking out of my life some 40 years earlier came crushing down on me like a lead weight, and I felt like I couldn't breathe. This wasn't a new memory, but my repressed emotional pain welled up and made me wonder once again, *How could he just walk away and leave my four sisters, my mother and me?* I had worked on these issues of abandonment and lack of male support and affirmation for much of my adult life, but in that moment I felt like I'd made no progress at all.

As I explored my feelings in my lonely bed that night, I realized that, even though I thought I'd resolved those memories, the emotional pain was still there, and it still continued to play a significant role in my life. The emotional wounds from my parents' divorce were still undermining my self-image and self-confidence, and now even my physical health. An intuitive feeling came over me that, by wearing the breathing machine, I was creating a justification for my husband to abandon me. Would my new fear become my reality? I became determined to heal my emotional wounds permanently and turn my self-limiting beliefs around, so I could heal my body and enjoy all the closeness I wanted with my husband.

In my 30 years as a physical therapist and an ergonomist (someone who reduces stress and prevents injury), I had long been seeing connections between clients' emotional pain and their physical symptoms. I understood how our unresolved emotional wounds could be the root cause of our physical ailments and how painful emotional events or memories could potentially harm our bodies. My sleep apnea was like other physical symptoms—an outward representation of my inner emotional pain.

The question is, how do we prevent our emotional wounds from continuing to hurt us? Many of us avoid experiencing and expressing our emotions, and instead discredit or suppress them. Sadly, these behaviors create physiological changes within our body that negatively affect our health, vitality and happiness, so that approach clearly doesn't work.

We also unconsciously alter our painful memories, behaviors and beliefs in order to shield ourselves from additional pain. We build walls of protection and defense mechanisms to ensure that we won't suffer again. This becomes what I call a "vicious dis-cycle of self," where emotional wounds create dis-satisfaction, dis-function, and dis-ease and become the fuel of our self-limiting beliefs. Depending on the intensity and energy of the emotional pain, we build taller and thicker protective walls, and stronger defensive behaviors that isolate us and create more toxicity within our bodies.

Understanding that *we created our self-limiting beliefs from our emotional pain* is integral to healing those emotional wounds and reclaiming our power. When we remove the energetic fuel of our painful beliefs, the emotional fire can be extinguished, and we can lower the walls of protection and stop the dysfunctional mental reruns of past traumas, never to be seen again. I've found over and over again that healing occurs in the body when you release your emotional pain from within.

When I experienced this vital link personally and also saw it professionally, I thought, *This is great! If we created our limitations and physical ailments, we can un-create them!* There is much research out there that supports the idea that our thoughts, words and emotions impact everything in both our internal and external world. In Japan, Dr. Masaru Emoto showed that water infused with negative thoughts, emotions, sounds or images formed ugly and deformed ice crystals, while water exposed to positive influences formed beautiful and symmetrical ice crystals. Given that 80 percent of our bodies consist of water, we can see how the quality of that water affects our health.

Also, in the U.S., Dr. Bruce Lipton's work on stem cell research confirms that you can influence what kind of cell a newly forming cell becomes (including how healthy it is) simply by altering its *environment*. So, if we can impact our internal chemical and hormonal environment in a positive or negative direction, clearly we can affect the health of our body, too.

These two examples illustrate the powerful effect that our emotions, thoughts and environment have on our bodies. Our emotional triggers can include pain, depression, anxiety, fear, PTSD, abandonment, rejection, lack of love… the list is endless. I'm sure you've experienced some emotional wounds and can see how they may be impacting you physically, mentally and spiritually. Releasing those old emotional triggers is critical to your emotional and physical health today, and so, too, is living a life in the present being authentic to yourself.

I've coined the term "the House of Emotional Pain" for the area within your body where your painful emotions reside and physical ailments or discomfort may be experienced. Your House of Emotional Pain could be anywhere, including the stomach, head, throat, heart, neck, shoulder, back, hip or groin. The location is not important; clearing out the painful emotions is.

Here is a powerful meditation tool called "the Heart's Home of Healing" that will cleanse your House of Emotional Pain of the emotional pain residing there. This meditation uses the power of your mind to transfer suppressed or trapped emotional pain to a very special organ in your body: the heart. In your heart, the pain can be experienced, released and replaced with love, light and joy. Please don't doubt that your emotional pain, whether from many years ago or just yesterday, is having detrimental effects on your happiness, health and harmony, and it must go—and it *can* with this simple technique!

Since your heart is *the seat of your soul* and the organ that is capable of emotional feeling, you must engage it to: 1) release your suppressed emotional pain, 2) initiate healing and 3) reestablish your energy flow. I created the Heart's Home of Healing Meditation to do this, and to provide what I call "steps of release and love to heal your pain." I encourage you to use this meditation often and enjoy profound relief from your old, accumulated pain and freedom from new pain. To listen to the audio version of this meditation, please go to www.CynthiaMazzaferro.com/HeartHomeofHealingmeditation.

The Heart's Home of Healing

1. Sit or lie comfortably with legs uncrossed in a quiet and secluded space.
2. Close your eyes and take three to five deep, slow, cleansing breaths (in through the nose, out through the mouth), emphasizing the exhalations. With each exhalation, release any stress, anger or frustration, and with each inhalation, breathe in peace, happiness and healing.
3. Identify *one* element—a belief, memory, emotion, symptom/illness— that you want to focus on during this meditation.
4. When you think of this element, where in the body do you feel it as a discomfort? This area is your House of Emotional Pain.
5. Assign a number to indicate the intensity of your symptom in that area now (1 low, 10 high).
6. Bring your attention to moving the discomfort from its current location into your heart.
7. Assign a number to indicate the discomfort you are experiencing now in the heart (1 low, 10 high). Often the number can change between the two locations.
8. Envision your heart, which has four chambers and four valves, as a house with four rooms, a central hub and four doors leading into those rooms.
9. Step into the central hub of your heart space through the front door. This area is the *seat of your soul*.

a. **Step A:** Enter the first room, notice the feeling within the room and express that emotion with a word. Then gather up whatever is in the room that you know does not serve you well—such as emotions, objects or people—and place them outside the window.

b. **Step B:** Turn and observe the room and notice if anything is still present that doesn't feel good. Gather it up and once again place it outside the window.

10. Walk through the door into the second room and repeat steps **A** and **B** in this room.

11. Enter the third and fourth rooms and repeat steps **A** and **B** in these rooms.

12. Now that you have cleansed the four chambers of your heart, move into the inner sanctum, the core, the *seat of your soul.*

13. Rest in this space, hear your beautiful heartbeat and notice how your pain has been greatly reduced or eliminated.

14. Standing in this central space, the core of your existence, allow the winds from the north to enter through the north window, the east winds from the east window, south winds from the south and west winds from the west. Let them all converge in your inner sanctum where you experience the clean, purified air and hold your intentions of health, harmony and happiness.

15. The Heavenly Source (north) enters your crown chakra from the top of the head, filling you with abundant grace, love and peace.

16. Feel the warmth under your feet or supported body from Mother Earth (south), as her nurturing and healing energies cascade upward into your heart.

17. Imagine these two energies from Heaven and Earth joining together to form a divine pillar of healing light that permeates the chambers of your heart and your whole body with every beat of your heart.

18. Observe how all energies merge and flow effortlessly throughout your being, completely filling your heart with love and healing light.

19. Rest and observe this inner space you hold, your heart space, and give gratitude for the release of all the emotional, mental, physical and

spiritual pain that you have removed from your physical body and your divine being.

20. Return to the rooms, starting with the last room and moving counterclockwise until you end up in the first room, shutting each of their respective windows as you go.

21. Your body and soul are abundantly full, and only health, harmony and happiness reside within you.

22. You may now leave your Heart's Home, feeling refreshed and knowing you can return as often as you would like, to be replenished and restored with love and light whenever you feel the need.

23. Take three to five slow, relaxed breaths and allow your attention to return to the present moment, moving your body parts and opening your eyes as you feel ready.

24. Observe the original pain location and once again assign a number. You most likely will see that the number has been greatly reduced or is zero.

The Heart's Home of Healing meditation has proven to be so powerful that many have experienced a profound shift and healing. But it's not a one-time practice. This meditation is a tool for healing the past *and* present, and should be used as often as needed until your emotional pain, mental limitation and energetic connection have been resolved. As you rehabilitate one element of concern, be aware that others may become evident.

Understanding how powerful your mind can be is quite liberating—and encouraging. Have you ever heard teachers or healers talk about the importance of letting go and wondered, *Okay, but how? It's not that easy!* See if this meditation doesn't do the letting go for you. It's certainly worked for me and many others. Once I freed myself from the emotional pain I had carried for so long, I lost 60 pounds, regained my health and happiness, and, oh yes, eliminated my sleep apnea. Hallelujah!

The day I returned the breathing machine to my doctor, he said, "You look like a different person! How'd you do it?"

"Oh, just some internal housecleaning," I said with a chuckle. He wanted to know my secret, so his other patients could reap the same rewards, and I told him all about The Power Within. I hope that, someday soon, doctors will be prescribing a deep cleaning of each patient's House of Emotional Pain just as routinely as they're prescribing pills today!

Remember, *you* hold the key to your Heart's Home of Healing. You can create a beautiful, healthy and love-filled life when you live from your inner sanctuary, the seat of your soul, the core of your heart. That's where The Power Within resides, and health, happiness and harmony are always present and available to you, enabling you to be Powerful Beyond Measure.

Cynthia Mazzaferro is the author of Powerful Beyond Measure: 3 Steps to Claim Your Power Within for a Happy and Healthy Life. *Learn the three essential steps to explore your past, empower your present and envision the future of your dreams. A transformational life coach, healer and highly sought-after motivational speaker, Cindy offers numerous programs and workshops on Powerful Beyond Measure and The Power Within.*

Her Emotional Health and Wellness Program teaches six powerful steps to eliminate emotional pain and self-limiting beliefs and gain a healthy range of E-Motions that will promote personal freedom, authenticity and self-expression. Find it at www. CynthiaMazzaferro.com.

Learn more about discovering your Power Within and becoming Powerful Beyond Measure at www.cynthiamazzaferro.com/powerful-beyond-measure-book.

To receive your **free** *weekly Powerful Beyond Measure Intuitive Soul Messages, visit her Facebook page, The Power Within Cynthia Mazzaferro.*

Cindy lives in Cheshire, Connecticut, with her husband and loves visiting her grown sons and their families.

Chapter 8

From Sleepwalking Through Life
to Traveling on a Jet Plane
Jannie Bak

Here's the trouble with life: you're halfway through it before you realize it's a do-it-yourself thing! For some people, love, success and happiness seem to fall out of the sky. For the rest of us, we're the only ones who can make something great of our lives. And a good place to start is to take a look back at what got you where you are today. Looking back, I can see that I never even asked myself the most important question: "What do *you* want of life, Jannie?"

Truth be told, it never occurred to me. I had been raised to be quiet and fit in and not make any fuss about myself. I was never asked what I wanted of life and I never even wondered. Basically, I didn't feel responsible for my life. I was just going along with it.

How about you? Are you letting your life slide by? Are you sleepwalking through life?

When you go to sleep tonight, you'll have one less day in the hourglass of your life. Are you spending those days wisely? Purposefully? Are your choices making you feel vibrant and alive? I was in my mid-40s before I woke up and asked myself these questions. But when I did, my life took off, as if suddenly I was riding on a jet plane. I have never told my story to anyone—not even my family. But let me share it with you now, and, hopefully, your life will take off, too.

I was not a wanted child; I was an "accident." Abortion was not an option in those days in Denmark, and even though my unwed mother was desperately climbing flights of stairs and jogging till exhausted to try to get rid of me, I had other plans and was born in January 1958. My parents were young and had to marry or be social outcasts. But my mother didn't love my father, and she still wanted to have her freedom and enjoy her life, so she divorced my father before I was a year old. I didn't meet him again until I was 12.

I grew up a lonely child. My mother married again and didn't tell me that Ole (pronounced like "Ola") wasn't my real father till years later. But I always had the feeling that he wasn't—and also that my mother wasn't my real mother! I remember lying in my bed at night, thinking that someone had left me in a basket on their doorstep.

Ole was violent and addicted to alcohol, and I was afraid of him. When I close my eyes today, I can still recall the times when he hit my mother and I cried and tried to stop him. He would push me away and yell that I'd be sent to a home for orphans if I wasn't quiet. He also beat me when we were alone. He'd tell me to keep my mouth shut or he'd send me to a foster home, so I never told my mother.

I loved my mother and looked to her for love and appreciation, but I didn't find it, until one evening when she was giving me a bath in the kitchen sink when Ole was out of town. She gasped when she saw my body, marked with blue bruises, and asked me what had happened. I remember her beautiful green eyes looking directly into mine. I stammered something like "I fell down at kindergarten." I did not want to be sent to a foster home.

She looked at me in a funny way.

"Jannie," she said. "I believe you're not telling me the truth. What has happened?"

I whispered back that Father had beaten me, and I was not allowed to tell, and now he would send me away forever. And then I cried.

Suddenly, my mother really saw me, as if for the first time. She hugged me, kissed me and told me she loved me and everything would be okay. She told me to go and dress myself and pack my favorite doll, Bella, with the blue velvet jacket. She quickly packed a suitcase and then grabbed my hand, and soon we were sitting in a taxi, heading for Grandma's house at the other end of Copenhagen.

Most of the time thereafter I lived with my loving grandma, as my mother went back to live with Ole, even though he was abusing her, too. At one point he abused her so much that she saw suicide as the only solution. She took some pills and turned on the gas oven, but she was found and taken to the hospital, where she stayed for quite some time. I remember Grandma and I visited her there. I had no clue as to what was wrong—only that her eyes looked empty and sad, and I wondered if it was all my fault.

A few years later, my mother divorced Ole and took up a new life of parties on the weekends and lots of new men. These relationships always involved some kind of trouble, and I didn't fit into the picture, so I still stayed with my grandma.

Years passed and, at the age of twelve, I was called to the headmaster's office at school one day. I arrived to find one of my mother's sisters waiting for me. Aunt Tove asked me to sit down, and then she told me that my mother had passed away. I remember thinking that it wasn't true. My mother was too young to die—only 30 years old. It had to be a mistake. Maybe she had just escaped for a while. Maybe she would come back. Even after the funeral, I kept looking for her in the streets of the city.

I remember the little altar I made at my table: a black-and-white photo of my beautiful, smiling mother, her eyes sparkling. A dark red velvet rose next to the picture and a little candle. Oh, I adored my mum. And I prayed for her to come back to me, to hold me and tell me that she wanted me and she loved me.

My grandma officially became my guardian and life continued. Then one day Grandma asked me to sit down for a talk. She told me that my biological father, Mogens, had called her and asked to see me. I had no memory of ever seeing him—he had never been allowed to visit me after their divorce—so I was curious. It was arranged that he would visit the next day, when I came home from school.

I was startled when I walked in the door the next day and saw Mogens for what felt like the first time. It was like looking in a mirror! There was no doubt that this was my real father. We hugged each other—both of us a little shy and hesitant—and talked for a bit. In the following years, we spent some time together, but I was never able to connect with him heart to heart because he irritated me a great deal, probably because he mirrored me. Maybe we could have become close someday, but he was killed in a car accident when I was 21.

In the midst of all this loss, at least I had my grandma. She was a wonderful woman with a huge heart, and my best memories from my childhood are of being with her. She raised me to be a nice girl. We were from the working class, and she often told me to do my homework, get a good education and get a job. Best would be in a bank; then I'd be home safe; I'd always have a job. I was never encouraged to consider starting my own business or going to university, and I was never asked what *I* wanted of life. I only learned to behave, to fit in and not to make any fuss about myself. And for many years, I did as I was told.

And then, slowly, I began to wake up. And that happened partly because I began to look back.

Look Back and Wake Up!

You might ask, "Why is it important to look back at our earlier years? After all, we can't change the past!"

Well, yes, that's certainly true. And for years I never wanted to look back. I didn't want to feel those feelings of being unwanted ever again. But I've come to believe that if we are willing to go back and face the old stories, we might gain a better understanding of who we are and how we see ourselves. When I first looked back at my life over the previous 10 years or so, when I was in my 40s, I saw that I had become very cautious with people. I saw that I didn't want to love anyone too much because they might leave me, and then I'd feel the pain of not being wanted again.

Looking further back in time, later, I could see that this pattern had affected me deeply for most of my life. I saw that I was loaded with old stories that were keeping me from standing in my own light and believing that I was okay and had a purpose in life. And seeing that, I became motivated to look all the way back to my difficult childhood years.

Of course it was painful to look back at those early days. It took all my courage. It had been so much easier to try to forget about those sad events and pretend they had never happened. But I'm grateful that I had the strength to persevere because it has been an eye-opener. Now I understand my own motives for doing what I did then—and what I do now—at a much deeper level. Now I can let go of some of the heavy emotional baggage I had been carrying. I can walk on feeling lighter and happier.

Some people call the process of looking back a spiritual process. I just know that I have been awakening and growing and feeling something new evolving in my heart every day. More and more, I've been allowing my feelings—good and bad, happy and sad—and not just turning away from them. And as I've done this I've realized that life is all about love. As a child, I had hungered for love and always tried my very best to win my loved ones' attention and appreciation. But now I saw that I could give myself that love. I no longer needed to get it from them.

I learned to appreciate my own company, and today I love to have my own space and the time to just to be with myself in silence. Long walks in the forest with my two dogs bring me to a state of meditative stillness in which my mind gets clear and wonderful new insights pop up.

Today I'm grateful that I found the courage to go back and look at those days. The puzzle of my life makes sense to me now, and I understand why I am the Jannie I am. I urge you to allow yourself the time to go back down memory lane and learn from your own story—because we all carry stories that we project onto the present, often in ways that limit us. Now you have a choice.

You can ask yourself, "Am I seeing and living the truth, or something that's all in my mind?"

A Life Built on Love

Today, my choices are mine and I love my life. I'm married to a wonderful man who respects my free spirit and allows me to fly with no restrictions. I've been blooming in my career and surrounded by colleagues and friends wherever I go ever since I found the perfect fit for myself in the profession of network marketing. In this field, your success is based on your ability to reach out and help others to achieve exactly what they want. The more you help others, the more you receive, and I love that. I love training my colleagues, and I know in my heart that we're going to write history together.

I recognize that the real reason I'm feeling so happy these days is that I've found a place in life where I can fill up the gaps left in my heart from my childhood. Today I feel connected and appreciated, some days even loved by the whole universe. Oh, what a joy that is!

Today, I dare to say that giving and receiving love is my deepest motivation in all that I'm doing. Love is now at the center of my life. It's been a long process and my journey has just begun—there is so much more to learn! I'm deeply curious and excited to see what the future holds for me.

My wish for you is that you realize you don't have to be limited by what happened to you in the past. All that matters is to learn to love and appreciate yourself today and find a way to express that love every day, in your work and play, and in your relationships with others. If you sometimes wonder why you're feeling less love than you want to, or if you maybe feel like something is keeping you from pursuing your dreams, please consider allowing yourself to take a walk down memory lane. You might find important insights hidden along the way that will help you understand yourself at deeper levels and finally break through old limitations. And please don't hesitate to take this journey in the company of a trained counselor, especially if there was a high degree of trauma in your past.

When you live a passionate life based on love and guided by your own personal choices, you have so much more to offer—to your family, your friends and yourself. Believe me when I say, from my own experience, it is never too late to wake up and love yourself—and create the life that makes your heart sing.

Jannie Bak, vintage 1958, had a long career in sales and marketing and found her place in life when she was introduced to Lifewave, an American health-technology network-marketing company. A front-row motivational leader in Lifewave, she also enjoys public speaking on network marketing.

Jannie loves nature, her home, her friends and family, traveling and making new friends. She loves to grow and learn and is motivated not by money but by feelings. Happiness and love are her inner fuel in life, and her dream is to help her friends and colleagues succeed and to inspire thousands of people to live their personal lives with joy and passion.

The mother of two sons and grandma of three, she lives with her husband, Bjarne, in the lovely countryside of Soroe, Denmark, and greatly enjoys the freedom of working from home. Connect with Jannie at www.janniebak.dk.

Chapter 9

The Golden Thread
Dipika Delmenico

The Pacific Ocean glistened as I took in the beauty of the California day from the sandy beach. It was my 29th birthday. That night, to celebrate, I had a glamorous evening on the town with my boyfriend, Steve, and friends that lasted into the wee hours of the morning.

Lying about in bed the next morning, I was reading a letter that had arrived from my father. Beside me, Steve, who was a foreign-correspondent journalist, was dutifully reading the round of daily newspapers, when suddenly, without any forewarning, he slumped forward, unconscious. It was a heart attack. Steve was a youthful 47; this couldn't be happening.

I moved through the next minutes and hours with a consciousness that was alien to me. Each movement was heightened and filled with fear: calling 911, doing CPR to try to resuscitate Steve, seeing the paramedics arriving and working on him. I was watching it all through a haze of shock and terror—and yet also with a deep, subtle all-knowingness: Steve was dying. This was real. I was living this.

The paramedics took Steve to the hospital, and I was not allowed to ride with them. An angel appeared to me in the form of a neighbor I'd not yet met, who drove me to the hospital behind the ambulance. Then I found myself sitting alone in a room in the hospital. A team of doctors and medics entered. They were somber.

"Steve is dead," one said. "We couldn't resuscitate him." My head dropped down between my knees, and the world as I knew it was smashed to smithereens.

The following days and weeks were a blur as arrangements were made to return home to Australia. I dulled the pain with alcohol as I moved through the days. Each night I longed for sleep to take me away. Each morning, sharp pain returned with my first waking breath.

I went about my life. Twelve months later, the cracks began to appear. I experienced anxiety, then my first debilitating panic attack. I made it through every day slowly and with great fragility. I wrote a list of even the simplest tasks, summoning all my courage to do them.

A dear friend encouraged me to participate in a meditation event with her. I declined, as I was afraid of falling further into the abyss of my despair. However, grace was gentle and benevolent. In my dreams, I would see a great Being in the room with me when Steve died. This Being's golden hand would take mine and lead me out of the gripping fear and darkness consuming me. It would lead me into light and hope.

One morning, upon waking after one of these dreams, I felt clearly what I had to do. I called my friend and said, "Yes, now I'm ready. I want to participate in the meditation event."

Once there, I discovered I felt light pulsate through me during meditation. I experienced love for myself like never before. I felt I had met my spiritual teacher, and, before long, I was living in an ashram in rural India, where my life took on a whole new trajectory. I was held by a daily rhythm that I've come to understand is the very foundation of authenticity and freedom. I was dancing within, feeling spiritual blockages being removed, as I grew stronger and took in new life.

But physically, embedded debris remained. During my grief and trauma, I had become so unable to digest my experiences that material sludge had accumulated in my body, clogging my mental, emotional and reproductive channels. I had no menstrual cycle for 18 months, and it seemed that my own inherent, potent power of womanhood had been cut off.

Time passed and, fortunately, I was led to a great healer, Dr. Ram Bhosle, a physician to Mahatma Gandhi. He was in his 80s and blind. I called him in Mumbai, and he greeted me like a long-lost friend.

"Ah, finally. I have been waiting. When are you coming?"

I went to him. I sat on the floor and he chatted away, tapping up and down my spine, over my reproductive organs. I exploded with pain inside but trusted implicitly that I was where I was meant to be, and this was safe. After that treatment, I left his home on Malabar Hill and looked out over the ocean. It was sparkling. I was sparkling. Everything was sparkling brightly.

The following day my menstruation began again. *Hello, my dear friend. I love you. I missed you. I am well.*

After a second extended term of service at the ashram, I returned to Melbourne, knowing it was time to resume my worldly duties. Soon, I fell in love again, but this was a different love. I was different. I had grown through my grief. I inherited two young boys, aged five and seven, whose birth mother had died after a long journey with cancer. We expanded our family, having three more children together.

Life was intense but full of grace, and I could see the golden thread that had woven through my journey thus far. It held me; it sustained me; it fed my connection to God.

This golden thread continues to weave from one junction to another in my life. At times, it's buried under my fatigue and inability to feel anything clearly, but I know it's there. It's pulsating subtly to remind me of who I am, and it's ready for me to follow it and fulfill my life purpose.

But life got tougher, and I struggled with raising an angry, unhappy teenage stepson. Often there was little sleep, and I was juggling so many balls in the air, with babies, nappies, teenage issues and demanding work. I felt desperate to maintain intimacy in my marriage, but I would go to sleep each night painfully aware of the lack of time or energy to nourish it. Friends told me I was a deeply good person and mother, yet I would cringe at fairy tales, questioning whether I had become the evil stepmother some of them portray.

Despite my daily meditation, prayer and yoga, the demands of my overly full life were taking a toll. I was serving as managing director of an international distribution business, running my clinical Ayurvedic practice and raising my family—and it wasn't sustainable. Plus, I worried that my teenage stepson, now dealing with mental health issues and addictions, was seeing us live in a daily state of crisis. Fear was eroding my well-being.

Then, at age 47, I had a health crisis. I thought it was perimenopause, but it turned out I was so disconnected from my own rhythms that I was nine-and-a-half-weeks pregnant and didn't know it until I was hemorrhaging and lost consciousness. I discovered I was pregnant as I miscarried. How could that be? I was a mother who had prided herself on being connected to the cycles of her own body! And a health practitioner!

My life force was gushing from me, and I didn't know how to stop it. I hovered above the scene in the emergency room of the hospital as they pulled out all the stops. Many staff rushed about me and I felt detached, peaceful, so close to God.

I was stabilized and I recovered, but I had to find a new way of being. The life force that had flowed from me had to be replenished. And, even in this physically weakened state, I could see the golden thread, illuminating the links of events in my life thus far, all leading me to my own unique purpose.

What is this golden thread that has always been within me? I see it as a thread of consciousness that is anchored in my heart, fed by cosmic forces from above and mineralized by earthly forces from below. It is moved by the life-giving force of each breath, inward and outward.

This thread is composed of truth, and its task is to guide me.

As I felt into the quality and language of this thread of consciousness, I found myself, just months after dancing on the threshold of death, beginning to fully participate in what resonated and enlivened me to the core. I was finally pursuing both my passion and my sense of duty to be of true and meaningful service.

Today, I feel the subtle vibrations of this thread within and the strength and clarity it gives me. I continue to ask the questions "Why I am here?" and "What is my life purpose?" And I've learned that nature's prompts, while simple, are what provide the way for us to feel connected to our own thread. I identified seven prompts, treasures that have brought me health and wholeness, and I offer them to you now.

Seven Treasures for Clarity and Purposeful Living

Treasure #1: Establish Daily Routines and Maintain Them

Daily routines aren't always easily established or maintained, and many people resist creating them. However, we thrive on them. They're key to good health and clarity because they nurture your mind, making it more powerful and focused. They release reserves of energy, making you more motivated and enthusiastic. Here are some of the most important routines:

- *Get up early at the same time daily.* Between 5 and 7 a.m. there are natural atmospheric vibrations that make the unconscious mind fresh and open to positive energies. This makes you more able to hear your inner self.
- *Eat meals at the same time daily.* For example, eat lunch between noon and 1 p.m.; don't skip lunch and snack at 3 p.m. Your digestive fire is stoked on schedule and wants to be fed or it rages, causing havoc.
- *Establish good sleep patterns.* Get to bed and try to be asleep by 11 p.m. daily. This is the foundation for vitality, clarity, focus and motivation. Good sleep equals good living. Lack of good rest and sleep depletes and weakens digestive capacity and can make the entire metabolic function dull and sluggish.

Treasure #2: Begin Each Day with a Reflective Practice

Sit quietly, comfortably, checking in with yourself: *Good morning, dear friend. How are you today?* Be with your incoming and outgoing breath, and witness what comes up. Do not wrestle with your thoughts; just watch them. This is about being with yourself, observing, listening, letting your heart speak to you. It may not be words or a language you are familiar with, but you will understand.

- Know that within you are all the answers you'll need in your life. They reside in your heart, and you must simply turn your attention inward to find them.
- You may want to establish a regular practice of sitting in the same place each day.
- Resist checking your phone messages or emails before you do this practice. Automatically checking messages upon waking is not a habit that's empowering you.

Treasure #3: Set Your Intention for the Day

In the reflective quiet of your morning ritual, ask yourself, *What do I want of this day? What are my priorities? What have I put off that I will address today?* This is doing your inner work, which cultivates inner steadfastness and clarity. The steps you take can be small, specific and scheduled, but set the big-picture intention first.

With this practice, you are able to *create* your life, instead of *reacting* to it and living under a blanket of expectations and obligations. The more established you become in this practice, the more intimate this dialogue and relationship can become. Your heart will speak truthfully, clearly and purposefully. Purpose is something we are born with, but can forget and lose connection with at times in life.

Treasure #4: Cleanse Regularly to Keep Digestion Strong and Bright

Good digestion is key to staying physically, mentally and emotionally well and authentic to yourself. Everything we eat and experience must be digested well for maximum longevity, intelligence, understanding and perception.

When your digestion is weakened, it's hard to have enthusiasm and energy for life. This is because a partially metabolized sludge builds up in the body and pollutes your thinking and feeling. Regular cleansing penetrates these blockages, mobilizing and eliminating sludge and preventing the accumulation of more.

Here are some gentle ways to cleanse:

- Fast on mung bean soup or vegetable soup one day a week, and for half a day when you have eaten heavily or not digested well.
- Sip ginger tea regularly through the day and particularly before and after meals.
- Take a gentle purgative of one teaspoon of castor oil before bed each night.

Treasure #5: Move Your Body

Your body is designed to physically move on a regular basis: movement creates metabolic bliss. Walking, yoga, tai chai, swimming, any kind of exercise daily supports healthy metabolic processes. Too little exercise creates stagnation and too much can deplete you.

Cultivating the practices of daily reflection and regular cleanses suggested above will help you to know what exercise is appropriate for you and when. In general, don't exercise if you're unwell, and don't overexert in the hot sun. Instead, choose gentle, restorative exercise, like a walk or gentle yoga stretches. The same applies to menstruating women. Be gentle, rest, go within and exercise your inner life.

Treasure #6: Take Silence After Periods of Intense Energy Expenditure

Periods of silence create inner space, which is essential for the flow of knowledge that the body's marvelous network of communication channels and processes depends on. Flow of knowledge is the key, and this can only occur where there is inner space. Silence reestablishes and nourishes flow. Silence is not to be feared, dear busy-minded ones! In fact, our minds love silence, for it is our natural state.

A thread cannot go through a needle unless the space is created for it to pass through. Silence is that space, a doorway to new possibilities and unleashed potential.

Treasure #7: Find Daily Means of Creative Expression

To be well, we must give creative expression to our lives, and imagination is key here. With imagination, you can see a picture in your mind; with creative imagination you can create a picture. The key to creativity is to play with whatever you feel passionate about. Whether it's to build, cook, sew, paint, journal, write, dance, sing, surf, cycle, be of service to those in need, build an empire… the possibilities are endless. Only you can drive this process of giving artistic expression to yourself.

Reflecting on the events in my life, I can see the junctions that became the stitches of my story. Each experience was a catalyst of growth and an opportunity to transform, and the most painful and challenging experiences have been the biggest catalysts to connect me with myself and my spiritual source. When I was alone, frightened and feeling rejected when Steve died, I was also feeling the pulsating energy of my destiny. I now know that the moments of greatest pain and loss in my life have been just as valuable as the most joyful and expansive moments.

Today, I can clearly see the golden thread of consciousness that weaves the rich tapestry of my life and others'. It is cosmic and unbounded and also unique to each one of us. We each have our own quality of thread, style of weaving and signature tapestry. This is our purpose and our destiny. And this is what makes our lives golden: we are made of golden consciousness.

Dipika Delmenico is an Ayurvedic medicine practitioner and a naturopath, educator, mentor and author. She has practiced traditional holistic medicine clinically for over 20 years, treating thousands of patients globally with the ancient wisdom of Ayurveda for wellness in the modern world. She is the author of The Ayurvedic Woman *and creator of the health program,* The Radiant Woman: Absolute Vitality for the Second Half of Life.

Passionate about holistic health and healing through Ayurveda and anthroposophical medicine, Dipika has gone beyond knowing it works to taking the deep dive into how it works. Committed to renewal of ancient healing mysteries, she has developed the sensitivity to be able to use the ancient technique of pulse reading and observation to gain insight into a person's physical, emotional, mental and soul health.

Dipika lives and practices in a rural Surf Coast community in Victoria, Australia, and can be found online at dipikadelmenico.com.

Chapter 10

Meet Your Higher Self and
Discover Who You Really Are
Keiko Anaguchi

My grandmother's name was Kiyoe (pronounced "Kee-yoh'-ay"), and that's what I called her. She raised me in the small village of Sakai, Osaka, in Japan, because my parents started a new business in town and had to work day and night to make our living. Kiyoe was born in 1899, and we shared the same birthday and zodiac sign, which is rare and not by chance. She was such a spiritual person that she could appreciate anything that took place in her life, good or bad, because she understood that good and bad are just illusions.

Every morning Kiyoe would sit in front of the family altar and chant mantras for our ancestors and thank them for protecting our family. She would say prayers for hours, and then she'd change the water and flowers on the altar. Then she would sit before a statue of the deity Amaterasu from the Shinto tradition and several icons, including one of the god of the house, and pray to each of them. She did this every day without fail.

Having grown up with Kiyoe's great example, I naturally developed my own spiritual practice. Up until the age of eight, I was very quiet and not at all sociable with my classmates. However, one day I heard a feminine voice very clearly and kindly say, "It is time now. You are safe here." At that moment, I happened to be watching other kids playing games in the school yard. Suddenly, I gathered up the courage to ask them, "Can I play with you?" In the next moment I was in the middle of the group of kids playing together, and I was laughing and having fun. It was a miracle for me. On that day, my life shifted into one full of joy and happiness.

I now recognize that that was the first time I heard my higher self speak to me. It seemed natural but also very special and precious. Since that day, I've chosen to listen to the many words of wisdom coming from my higher self, which have dramatically improved my life. Visits from my higher self became more frequent as I got older, maybe because I appreciated them so much. More recently, they have led me to create an organization called Dynavision that provides spiritual training programs in Japan to help people become awakened and find true happiness through connecting to their higher selves.

The first time I actually saw my higher self, I was a young woman working at my first job. I happened to be playing tennis at the time. I had been working a lot and was so tired that I was standing on the line just trying to summon the strength to serve. Suddenly, my mind was filled with white light, and when it faded, I saw my higher self standing right next to me on the court. I turned to her and saw that she was formed in my image but made of pure white light. She was smiling kindly at me, and I felt bathed in love. The experience was thrilling, and at the same time it felt very natural. After a moment, she merged into my body, my mind became crystal clear and my energy returned. I served well and won the point, and eventually the game.

That day I realized that my higher self is here to help me experience the best possible life, as is true for everyone. This and other similar experiences inspired me to dedicate my life's work to helping people connect and communicate with their higher selves. Would you like to gain that knowledge? The first step is to be open to the possibility of all good coming into your life. Please take a moment to consider these questions deeply:

Can you imagine knowing why you were born?

Can you open to the possibility of being capable of manifesting whatever you want?

Can you welcome the idea of having unlimited choices in life?

Can you see yourself as worthy of receiving abundance?

I believe you can have all of this and much more. Your higher self naturally radiates an all-encompassing joy because it exists in higher dimensions where love is all that exists. It is directly connected to Source and has access to limitless energy and understanding. It embodies oneness and is intimately connected to All That Is. Your higher self is happiest when it is able to pass all of its love, energy and joy on to you because it loves you and is eager to give you the knowledge you need to raise your vibration, find joy and spread love in the world. Your higher self is there to open all doors of possibility and to co-create with you the highest possible outcomes in your life.

The only obstacles to your receiving all of this abundance are your feelings of unworthiness, your lack of self-love and your misunderstanding about who you really are. The wonderful thing is that your higher self is always with you and never judging you, no matter what mistakes you make. It's always supporting you and nudging you to grow in the direction of giving and receiving all good.

I sometimes hear my higher self say things like "Keiko, we are one, we are always together, so why don't you trust me even more?" This might be after I make a decision based not on what my higher self suggests but on what my ego wants. But whatever mistakes I've made, I've never felt judged by my higher self whatsoever, even if I don't follow the suggestions she lovingly provides. And I say "she" because even though, in reality, our higher selves are gender neutral and totally balanced between masculine and feminine energies, at times they will appear to us as a specific gender so that it's easier for us to identify with them.

The purpose of your higher self is to help you embody light and love to the highest degree possible. It does this by assisting us in fulfilling our soul's mission on this planet and by helping us become more complete. No matter where we are in our evolution, our higher selves help us continue to evolve, even though, from our perspective, they mostly reside in a different dimension.

The love your higher self has for you is eternal and unconditional. All you have to do is tune in to it. I do this through meditation and, when I am having a particularly difficult experience, through my strong intention. That is when my higher self comes through most powerfully—to help me navigate trying times and maintain my high vibration and sense of equanimity.

It may be difficult to imagine, but the power of your higher self is limitless. That doesn't mean you can use it to do whatever you want, though. It means that all of the power of the universe is available to you when you're engaged in action that is for your highest good and the highest good of everyone involved.

Since your higher self is directly connected to Source, its power flows freely from Source. Your higher self has no real form because it is an energetic being. This gives it the ability to appear to you in different forms, depending on what's easiest for you to relate to in a particular moment. Sometimes my higher self takes a form resembling an Egyptian goddess, such as Isis, which makes me feel powerful and passionate and able to move forward easily. When I need to be still and contemplate the situation more deeply, my higher self appears as Mother Mary.

I have developed a deeper connection to my higher self through both studying and teaching at Dolphin Star Temple, a Mystery School in Mount Shasta, California, that was founded by the late Amorah Quan Yin. Through my work at Dolphin Star, I've reached a point where I can totally trust my higher self with every aspect of my life, having fully realized that we are one.

Your higher self can help you reach this level, too. It can pinpoint exactly what you need to focus on and how you can get the most out of each experience. When I'm facing a challenge, my higher self frequently helps me reorient myself and identify the lesson to be learned and what I can do differently in the future.

Since I've made the connection with my higher self, I no longer get confused by life because she tells me what's the best thing to do. As a result, I've become very creative and decisive. I no longer doubt my decisions, I'm more confident in myself and my creative abilities, and my power of manifestation has been multiplied by a hundred times, at least!

All higher selves have their own unique vibration, which can most easily be described as a color. The color of your higher self is an indicator of its purpose or mission. In my case, my higher self is pink-gold surrounding pink-purple, indicating that it's what I call a Love Manifestor, which means that I am serving my highest purpose when I create based on love. It's true that everything flows effortlessly when I'm in that state.

In order to experience the vibration of your higher self, use this simple practice on a regular basis:

1. First, quiet your mind by breathing deeply and focusing on each breath.
2. When you feel settled, call upon your higher self to come to you as a body of light.
3. Be aware that you may feel, see or sense that your higher self appears as a body of light in one or more colors, including white. Don't mind if you experience nothing. Just have the awareness that your higher self is present, and remain open to the possibility of seeing it.
4. Ask your higher self to merge with your physical body, and notice any changes that occur, physically or visually, again not minding if you perceive nothing.
5. If you have any experience, however subtle, take time to fully experience it as the presence of your higher self.
6. Once you can sense the vibration of your higher self, even if very faintly, you can ask it questions, such as the following:
   • How can I better serve my community?
   • What can I do to connect with you more deeply?
   • What is my life purpose?
   • How can I fulfill my life purpose?
   • What do I need to be aware of in order to spiritually awaken?

Our higher self is unique to us and has its own unique vibration, which appears visually as one or more colors—and this can change over time and in different circumstances. Its color indicates the purpose of our life at that time, as follows:

- **White** indicates the purpose of truth-seeking and bridging between heaven and earth. This person is peaceful and innocent, has an aura of purity and provides a tangible connection between the divine and the physical.
- **Yellow** is not a color of cowardice—just the opposite! One strong purpose of the person with this higher self is to help others express more courage and confidence in their lives.
- **Royal blue** is the expression of the divine. This higher self encourages the person to tune into their own divine nature, so they can express divinity in their own life and help others realize their own divinity.
- **Pink-purple** indicates the life purpose is to learn how to express unconditional love, compassion and mercy for themselves and for others.
- **Emerald green** carries the mission of gaining self-acceptance, expanding to accept others, accepting and loving what is, and letting go of illusion. It is often found in artists, musicians and writers.
- **Orange** energy in a higher self helps co-create wholeness on this planet using heightened senses and creativity. It can break up stagnant energy patterns and pave the way for powerful manifestation in the world.
- **Red** energy represents the frequency of action and the energy of cosmic fire that can burn up anything that's no longer needed. It provides the motivation to move forward with passions.

We often make the mistake of thinking of different frequencies as being higher or lower, but this isn't the case. Think of your higher-self color as if it were on a color wheel, where no color is better than another. They're all equal and together make up the whole.

It's also important to remember that the higher self doesn't actually have a form or color but just chooses to make itself known in that way to humans because we perceive through our five senses. For example, I experience Mother Mary as having a beautiful light blue color, Kuan Yin metallic lavender and Jesus a powerful red surrounding a unique rainbow of colors. Mother Theresa has a light yellow color and sometimes blue. The Buddha appears as a shade of orange, and Saint Germaine, as violet. Still, I understand that they are, in reality, formless and colorless.

If you would like to feel the vibration of your higher self and see its colors, practice embodying your higher self on a daily basis, as described earlier. To review, just sit easily, feel your body relax and let your mind be quiet. Then, simply have the intention to connect with your higher self. Be open and don't mind if nothing seems to happen.

Make time for this simplest of practices daily, and, over time, you will begin to feel connected with your higher self and see its colors, and your life will shift into the more harmonious reality you have always wished for. You will begin to make the best choices and decisions for your life path effortlessly. You will no longer need to wait for miracles to happen; instead, you will be the one who is the cause of many quiet miracles for both yourself and others. Being in tune with your higher self will take away fear and lead you to be happy and able to enjoy your life experience. Once your higher self is consciously embodied in your physical body, your vibration will become higher and higher, and you will attract great abundance.

Now it's your turn to take the opportunity to realize how magnificent you truly are! Please remember that you are no less than the Ascended Masters I have mentioned here. In your essence, you are equal to everyone, including any of the Masters you admire. And when you are in touch with your higher self, you become a creator of infinite potential. You remember that you are a beautiful and unique being of light who came to this planet to experience the highest possibility of creation. I urge you to seize every opportunity to pursue this worthy goal and enjoy the endless blessings of getting to know your higher self!

A well-known spiritual teacher, author and public speaker in Japan, Keiko is recognized for manifesting spiritual messages in realistic forms. Keiko channels Amaterasu, the divine feminine force of the Sun, also known as the bringer of light from heaven. She founded the Spiritual Entrepreneurs' School in Japan to teach people how to bring spiritual skills to everyday business life to shift the present reality to a new reality that better serves

humanity. Keiko is the bestselling author of various titles, including Find Your Own Angels *and* Law of Attraction: Life is Full of Miracles. *Serving over 25,000 clients in the past 20 years, Keiko also leads spiritual tours to Mount Shasta and Sedona in the U.S., as well as to other sacred sites around the world, including in southern France, Egypt and Peru. To receive a meditation that can assist you in embodying your higher self, please go to www.keikoanaguchi.tokyo.*

Chapter 11

From the Eagle Road:
Where Dreams Bring New Life
Maru Méndez

There are days that mark our very existence and change the course of what we thought was to be our journey. It was on one of these days that I decided to get away from events in my life that were bringing me much suffering.

I set off, not knowing what was in store for me. And it was on that journey, far from home, that I started to see things differently. While standing on a mountaintop, on a trail called the "Eagle Road," I listened to the words of an extraordinary man who would remind me of a basic lesson easily forgotten: when one dream dies, it makes way for another to be dreamed and fulfilled.

I had been privileged to receive a master of science degree at Stanford University, and, after I graduated, many doors opened for me in the executive world. While I pursued a business career, I chose the field of human development as my focus of ongoing study and inner work. After more than 10 years of courses, workshops and retreats in that field, I returned to Palo Alto to pursue a master's degree in transpersonal psychology, which enriched my experience as an executive in the corporate world in many interesting ways.

Because of my past, I always tried to understand human nature and, especially, the reasons why we sometimes cannot leave the past behind. When the highest executive position I had ever occupied (as marketing director in a pharmaceutical company) suddenly ended, I decided to go on a journey of inner discovery.

I took off across the seas to foreign lands. Spectacular landscapes surrounded me, but deep inside I was traveling through the land of those in mourning. The journey evoked sad memories of recent experiences and relationships. I cried. I thought. I was again in pain. Then came understanding, forgiveness and gratitude. And, later on, again I struggled with my memories. Then, stillness and once again the storm.

On the third week of my trip, I had an unforgettable morning. I sailed into the port of Geiranger, a small tourist village in the western part of Norway on a cruise ship filled with 3,000 people. I soon found myself on a bus to the summit of a magnificent mountain: Trollstigen. Upon reaching the peak, at Ørnesvingen viewing point, I stepped out and was absorbed by the grand vista of land and sea reaching to the horizon. A man stood in a clearing with a few people sitting near him. I would learn his name was Zion. I closed my eyes to better take in the spiritually charged atmosphere I was breathing. After a while, I decided to sit down and meditate. A few minutes later, with my eyes closed, I heard a woman on my right coming near.

This is how her dialogue with Zion began:

"Are you a healer?" she asked.

"I just make a few rituals," he replied. "What is it that fills your heart with pain?"

"How do you know?" she asked.

"Your eyes tell me so. What makes you so sad?" he said.

She started crying. "When will I be able to stop these tears?"

"Woman, you had better leave outside, and not inside, what is making you suffer."

"Sometimes there seems to be nothing that can stop this pain."

"That is a false idea. Welcome the expression of what gives you pain. The sooner the better, for that is the only way for you to understand what is making you so sad."

"Sometimes, after crying, I feel sadder."

"Then nobody has explained to you what your tears are for. At first, they cloud our vision, but when tears are released, they allow our heart to express what hurts."

There was silence for a few moments.

"I am Carissa," the woman said.

"And I am Zion," the man replied. "Come, Carissa, sit here."

She came and sat.

"I have lost everything."

"Have you really lost everything?"

"Perhaps not, but sometimes I don't feel strong enough to carry on. I can't stand this pain."

Again, there was silence. Then Zion said, "Carissa, feeling pain is part of our human experience. Pain is simply a signal, a message about thoughts or behaviors that need to be reconsidered. The problem is not feeling pain; it is failing to heed the message the pain is trying to convey."

"I still haven't received any message from this pain. I do not know what it is I should reconsider."

"When we lose something, there are two questions that help us know what needs to be reconsidered: What do you think you have lost? And what did you really want to get from it?"

After a moment, Carissa said, "I lost my husband."

"And what did you get from being with him?"

"Besides his presence, he made me feel loved."

"Carissa, where did you feel that love?"

"Obviously, here," said Carissa, touching her heart.

"If the love he made you feel was generated in your own heart, you can always feel it again."

"But he has gone."

"Yes, he left, but you still have your heart where you have what he taught you to feel: love."

I felt a stirring in my chest at these words. Zion went on: "You think you have lost everything, but you must realize that that is not true. We are unavoidably destined to lose whatever is inherently material. Although at first glance that might not seem encouraging, what *is* encouraging is to remember that there is nothing to stop us from fulfilling our greatest longings, for they are all of a nonmaterial nature.

"Many times we get stuck when contemplating a lost dream, but that is only because our perception has been limited, and we have forgotten to observe the full panorama of life with its countless options—the way an eagle would."

"I don't understand," Carissa said.

"Your partner was quite likely your dream come true."

"Yes, he was."

"And what is it you longed for with this dream?"

"I craved love," she replied.

"If feeling love was what you craved, you must learn that there are many other ways to generate it."

Then he continued: "Carissa, how long ago did the man who is still present in your heart and thoughts disappear from your sight?"

"It is almost a year since he left."

"You can take all the time you need to decide to put that chapter behind you, but there is something you should never forget: letting go of yesterday is an indispensable step toward setting in motion what is awaiting you."

"And how can I let go off yesterday?" she asked.

"Yesterday is over when you simply accept that what happened is in the past and, quite likely, because of what happened, you are a better person. Yesterday is over when you realize there is nothing to forgive, and you can be grateful for what occurred."

"But sometimes I cannot forgive."

"Only when you remember something that hurts you again."

"So how can I stop being hurt?"

"What usually hurts us the most are beliefs and thoughts that should be questioned before taking them for granted. You may think you have failed, but the only thing that has failed is your understanding of the meaning of this journey, for, in truth, we have come here to experiment. To learn. Did something end? Then accept that what is no more does not belong in your reality now, and trust that what is yours by birthright will come to you."

I opened my eyes in time to see Zion giving Carissa an eagle's feather.

"Why are you giving me this?" she asked.

"The legend says that, upon reaching the middle of their lives, the eagles shed their plumage and grow it anew."

"And do you think that is true?"

"I think that it does not matter whether something is or is not true, just like the problems that brought you here. What matters is the meaning we take away from what we have lived. May this feather always remind you of your freedom and your capacity to fly again."

Their eyes met. Zion said, "Do not forget: renew yourself. Change your clothes and throw away everything that reminds you of that time, which is now over."

She hugged him, and so it was farewell.

I breathed deeply, enjoying the silence that had fallen. As I began to get up in order to thank Zion for his revitalizing words, I saw that he was not there anymore. Where was he? I waited for him to appear, but he was gone. It would soon be time to get on the ship that would take me to my new destiny.

Later, I learned that this mountain is frequently visited by shamans, revered in indigenous traditions that existed long before our culture decided our bodies had to be healed separately from our mind and spirit.

Zion is a name which some say means "the highest point," the name of a man whose simple words began to change my perspective on life. In his absence, I soon understood what he had explained: we are meant to lose everything of a material nature, but the important thing is that we learn to accept "what is," letting go of what is gone and trusting that our birthright will come to us. I might never see him again, but his message will never be erased from my soul.

Back at Home

Some weeks later, I started rewriting my life. Further away from the emotional turbulence of that time, I began to process my experience with the eyes of a transpersonal psychologist. Zion's recommendations were a simple way to summarize so many lessons. First among them for me was: Why do I, or any of us, sometimes insist on trying to recover something that is no longer there, when there are so many other ships to take?

I noted three conditions that have made it hard to leave the past behind:

1. If I stop feeling and expressing my emotions, I cling to the past and only put off my suffering. Repressing emotions doesn't help.
2. If I become wedded to my thoughts, I am condemned to suffer from the apparent effects of past events.
3. If I only see what happened in the past, I limit my capacity to dream again. I look down instead of looking ahead or turning my eyes to the sky.

Find Emotional Release

Emotions are helpful messengers that our bodies use to point out issues we must confront. For me, finding a safe environment where I can express myself without consequences, restriction or judgments helps me face my true emotions. When you face your true emotions, it's good for your health: it normalizes blood pressure, modifies brain-wave patterns and improves your immune function.

Accepting your emotional reactions to events, rather than rejecting or repressing them, is the only door that takes you back to the best version of yourself. It's only from there that everything can be understood and solved in a better way.

Create an Emotional Profit and Loss Statement

As Zion reminded me, what usually hurts most are our beliefs and thoughts about the consequences of our past actions. When you question those beliefs and thoughts, you can change them.

I've found that a powerful way to do this is by creating an "Emotional Profit and Loss Statement" that summarizes the self-perceived gains and losses you've incurred in a given experience. This can be an effective way to question your false assumptions about the past. I suggest you make a form with the following headings:

The Emotional Profit and Loss Statement

As a result of this event that still causes me pain, I have the following losses and profits:

Losses: What I tell myself I have lost	Profits: What I tell myself I have gained

List as many points as you can under Losses and Profits, and soon you'll easily be able to identify your false assumptions, mistaken beliefs and overstatements.

Small Steps Can Activate Your Capacity to Dream Again

There are moments in life when it seems impossible to dream again. We get tired of thinking painful thoughts and can't find ideas or projects that might lift our spirits. But your ability to dream is stimulated through your right brain, not the logical left brain. So, engaging in right-brain activities, such as walking or dancing or contemplating the landscape, are of utmost importance in your recovery, for it's not through thinking that you'll begin to dream again but through feeling.

It might also be the case that you have set goals that depend for their success on getting the right response from others, who are not always ready to give us what we desire. Try flowing with whatever happens instead. Some Asian traditions, like the Tao, remind us of the importance of flowing with the natural progress of things, rather than forcing things to happen. And consider that sometimes your dreams do not materialize simply because you've limited the scope of your desires: unexpected paths can bring you more than you ever hoped for.

Final Thoughts

You can accept even painful experiences as valuable if you understand that they are there to expand your consciousness. To make such experiences more useful, consider these points:

1. If you're able to express the pain you've suffered, you'll have a better chance of gaining emotional liberation. For example, crying can be a valuable process that clears your vision to help you observe past events from a wider perspective and see a better future.

2. The act of stopping and facing whatever has happened, instead of pretending that nothing has happened, is essential to recovery. We have to stop fighting what happened and find a way to accept it, in order to let it go. This acceptance will allow you to receive the gifts the experience offers.

3. From a certain distance and a place of silence, you can gain clarity. Seeing things from the perspective of the Eagle Road means having the capacity to see beyond what is apparent and reconnect with the essence of life—something you'll surely overlook if you focus on your supposed failures and problems!

4. When you're in touch with the essence of life, you'll remember that you're surrounded by countless options and can always choose differently and dream again. You'll suffer less when you remember you'll always be able to create a new future for yourself.

5. Regaining the power to dream begins with simply giving yourself the chance to move the body (to activate the right brain) and acknowledge your wishes again. Wishing and dreaming may be the most important aids in leaving the past behind.

Zion's words showed me that, while I may have appeared to be running away from my difficulties when I took off on my journey, I was actually seeking to shift my attention toward release, renewal and the reimagining of my life. If you have had a loss, I urge you to stand up, reconsider the meaning of your experiences, embrace your desires and dare to dream again! When you do, you acknowledge that whatever seems to have been taken away from you was not the end of your journey. You'll discover that no matter what has happened, when you keep your eyes on your dreams, one way or another, they'll come true.

After receiving a master of science degree from Stanford University, Maru Méndez spent the first half of her professional journey as a business consultant and executive. Her early career was focused on business transformation, but as she managed large groups of people, she realized that the more significant challenges are in the field of human development. This discovery, along with personal challenges, sparked Maru's desire to start a new stage of preparation in the field of human development. Many wide-ranging disciplines were added to her résumé, including Inner Child Healing, Fear-Pain-Anger Management, Crystal Therapy and Kriya Yoga, plus becoming a Reiki master.

In 2013, Maru was granted a master's degree in transpersonal psychology by the Institute of Transpersonal Psychology. In May 2016, she published her first book, Vuelvo a mí [Back to Me], available in English and dedicated to those who wish to put the past behind them.

---- *Chapter 12* ----

Getting Back to Me:
How Loss Can Lead to Self-Discovery

Jennifer Dean

This is dedicated to all those who struggle for the right to love, to be who they are and want to be, and to live their lives in freedom, equality, diversity and respect, in a time when we are in the shadow of the Orlando massacre.

Do you ever look back on favorite times in your life? One of mine was 1997. I called it my "champagne year" because I always ordered a bottle of champagne when out on the town. That was the year I began producing theater events in collaboration with a performance poet in London. In the evenings I ran my theater production company, and on weekends I came home to the countryside to visit friends and my mother.

My day job was running my IT consulting business and working all over the U.K., designing businesses' security systems. Despite the fact that I had two jobs, there was always time for fun. I took flying lessons as a present to myself and went Christmas shopping in a different country, as I did every year. There were parties, concerts, theater events and festivals galore, and I loved every minute of it.

But all of that went away in 1998.

The year started out fine with rehearsals for a play that ran for three weeks in February. It was sold out every night and generated great reviews and all the excitement and parties that go with a hit show.

Then, one day in March, I was walking along a London street when I looked up and saw a steel cabinet falling almost on top of me. I had no time to run. I put my hand on my head and BAM! The lights went out. Then my eyes opened briefly to see my foot was trapped. And then another steel cabinet fell, hammering the first one into my foot. I felt the pain as the bone broke, then nothing.

I awoke in the hospital with pain everywhere and no control over most bodily functions. I had been hit all along my left side, on my head, shoulder, leg and back. My new mobile phone had been pushed into my ribs. The doctors stuck a pin in me and there was numbness all down my left side. A few weeks later, I left the hospital in a wheelchair with Mum holding the crutches I would need.

Weeks went by with Mum tending me. She would have to sit me up in bed, as my spine was weak and my left hand and shoulder gave way, but once sitting I could just about support myself. I could not lift a kettle or fill it, I had a permanent headache and mental fog, and I swallowed painkillers like they were sweets.

After two months in bed, I tried to go back to work using crutches. I had to work, as bills were coming in, and I thought some of the management duties at my IT company would be doable. But I couldn't cope with reading or writing— it was like seeing ants running across the page—or do mental arithmetic or speak properly. And the terrible shooting pain down my neck, spine and leg made it impossible to concentrate.

At home I looked at books and files, not knowing what to do with them. I couldn't sleep for more than two or three hours at night and felt disconnected from everything, including my mum. My cat would sit on my chest and look in my eyes, and I would look back blankly. I had no connection with the person I saw when I looked in the mirror.

It was a relief when I was finally diagnosed with cognitive problems and could begin treatment. I left my home and spent about six months at a brain rehabilitation unit, and then two years at another rehab center. In the beginning, I lost my ability to talk with others and felt confused and lost, being away from Mum. When the rehabilitation team tried to get me into a simple job, I saw a report that said, "Can do a few hours of filing but needs supervision." Something inside me sank. The knowledge that I had gone from running my own business to doing filing "under supervision" occupied my thoughts for many months.

I worked hard at relearning how to read newspapers and books and do day-to-day tasks with strategies I developed using color, Post-it notes and alarms. And finally, after two and a half years, enough of me was functioning for me to be able to get back into the world. I remember the check I got on the test paper for correctly "going to a telephone, answering it and saying 'hello.'"

At 42, I was too young to stop work and give up on my life, but I couldn't resume my former career. So, I went back to university. I took the bus and went to class on crutches and heavy pain medication. I used a voice recorder as my hand couldn't work fast enough to take notes. At home I would listen to the voice recording in bed, replaying every lecture like a song until eventually I would remember it.

I was in a special study group in which we recited the answers to each other until we remembered them. During the exams, I had three hours' extra time with breaks to stretch and ease the pain. By the end, my hand would be in such pain it would stop working and have to be rested all the next day. Nonetheless, I got stronger and increased my mobility. I reduced my "brain shutting down" time and slowly improved my stamina.

But then a whole new problem arose. The strong painkillers I'd been taking had delayed the discovery that a disc had gradually been projecting farther and farther into a nerve in my back, creating increasing pain. At this point, there was no known treatment for this, so at the start of year two I was sent home, totally bedbound, with intensely painful sciatica and back pain.

Ever since the accident, I had felt deeply inadequate, less than whole. But now, being bedbound at home in London, I was also isolated. I couldn't bear to have old friends see me this way or to try to socialize to find a relationship, as I didn't think anyone would want to go out with me, anyway. I felt like a failure. I was surrounded by a life I used to live, and I couldn't relate to that life. I had become a person who could hardly stand, walk, speak properly or hold a conversation. Who was I? And would I always be alone?

Through the window, I could see the leaves on the trees changing through the seasons. After months of lying in bed in pain, watching the leaves, with my mother and physiotherapist as my only visitors, one thought began to occupy me: *just swallow all the tablets and end it all.* There was no joy, laughter, fun or love. My life had become the size of my bedroom.

But the next thought stopped me: *Who would look after Mum?* I felt it was my responsibility. Mum came twice a week to sit with me, talk to me, hold my hand, touch my forehead, brush my hair, clean me up and change my clothes. And someday she would need me.

The physiotherapist said people could recover, and she wrote down a website about someone who had reduced her sciatica pain through exercise. Reading this was a revelation. I made a choice: I would keep the pain and my life, and exercise however I could. When I could sit up for 10 minutes, I progressed to 20 minutes and then tried standing. When I could stand for twenty minutes, I had a shower.

Close to my window was a post box, and posting a letter became my new goal. I made the journey in my mind every day for a couple of weeks, and then, one day, I wrote my name and address on a card, put a stamp on it and set out to post it. It took nearly 20 minutes, and some of the way I was crawling, but finally I crashed into the letter box to rest. I had made it! Never mind that it took another twenty minutes to get back to bed—I had achieved my goal!

I felt a deep inner joy. For the first time, I loved my injured, disabled, pain-racked body. I loved my mind, damaged as it was, and even my lack of a personality and identity. I was still here, and I could get better.

In the coming days, I often thought about the people I had seen at the post box. They were not alone like me, and many walked hand in hand. Love is important.

I had been thinking, *How could anyone love me, damaged as I am?* I was single and gay, which isolated me further. But now I saw something. Somehow, for years, I had put so much energy into my work and my family and their views about my being gay that I had let that part of my life remain empty. Being the youngest, I had thought from an early age that my duty was to look after my parents. Maybe that's when I stopped loving myself enough to give myself what I really needed. Now, I knew I had to learn to love my body with all its physical limitations. I had to learn to love and accept myself for all of me.

Finally, I was on my journey back to me. I didn't know what I might be able to be or do, but I knew I had to find my way to a good life.

Slowly, over the next four years, I retrained in law and built a new career in employment and business law. After another three years, I became head of legal and personnel for a group of nine companies. Today, I run my own business and have contracts with many organizations. I also began to date and rebuilt my confidence in that area.

For many years, I still carried the fear that I could become bedbound again at any time, so I kept going to the gym. I worked so hard at it that I eventually qualified as a fitness trainer! I use that knowledge today to help myself and others balance exercise and work life, and, truly, each is equally important to me.

I learned that the brain is amazing! It can build new neurological pathways, and it *will* find new ways to learn and remember if you can just keep at it. The mind and body can work together to support healing. This human form we have is where we live, so we have to look after it, nurture it and, most of all, love it.

Here are six simple steps that sum up what I had to do to regain an active mind and body and to grow to love myself more every day. Please consider trying them in your life and breaking all your boundaries and limitations, just as I did.

Step #1: Set an Intention; Have a Goal

Even if you just set a small goal at first, it will help motivate you to do what you set out to achieve. I set a big goal—to be able to return to my normal work life within three years of going back to college. But to do that I also had to set a series of microgoals, one after another. The first one was to be able to sit up in bed by myself and then stand up for more than three minutes. I set my intention, I held my vision in my mind's eye, I lived it and breathed it, and then I took action.

Step #2: Write Down What You Want to Achieve

Whether in a notebook or on Post-it notes or a big poster on the wall, write down your goals and look at them daily. I used Post-it notes and had them everywhere—on my books, my bedside table, my phone, my front door, even on the walls. And I still use them today. But you might want to keep a journal or a video diary. Use whatever you feel comfortable with and can easily see every day. Keep looking at it and updating it. Keeping a diary or journal is great because you can look back and see your progress and be inspired by how far you've already come.

Step #3: Keep Learning and Do Something New Every Day

To keep your mind active and agile, try new things, whether it's learning a new language or taking up a new hobby, such as gardening or doing crossword puzzles or whatever! Your brain is like a muscle and it needs exercise. Whether you're in recovery or pursuing goals in your everyday life, you need to keep focused and use all your mental potential if you're going to make serious progress.

Step #4: Do Not Give Up on Yourself!

Believe in yourself and act out your belief every day. Look in the mirror and look deep into your eyes and say, "I can do this! I will succeed!" My hardest challenge was learning to walk again after being bedbound. It was painful and exhausting, but I kept saying over and over and over, "You can do this! You can't give up!"

Step #5: Keep Moving and Use Music

Just go walking, stretch your body, go out dancing, enjoy the music, or dance at home for 20 minutes every day. Take brisk walks every day and invite a friend! Movement and conversation or music can help change your mood, thoughts and energy levels.

Step #6: Be Your Authentic Self

Be true to who you are, and you will be happier with yourself and the lifestyle you are choosing, with or without disabilities. Every time you make the choice to show up honestly in the world, as exactly the person you know you truly are, you become stronger and happier. This is the one true path to a fulfilling life. I finally came out to my mum, and today she is almost as fond of my beloved partner as I am. People can change! And love smooths the way.

Remember this: you are stronger than you know. Whatever obstacles you encounter, know that you can come back from them and regain a good life. Let me tell you from experience, you can lose a great deal, even your mind and mobility, but with enough determination and hard work, you can gain back much, if not all, of it, or, if necessary, find peace with the loss as it is. Life is too precious to ever give up on.

And maybe just as important, you can also find the strength to make any hard or brave choices you need to make. Believe me when I say that the joy of living an honest and loving life will make all your efforts worthwhile.

Jennifer is a semi-retired barrister at law in London, specializing in working with low-paid union members. Combining a science background with law, she sits on a national environmental committee and also has a business consulting company. She serves as chair of law at the British Computer Society and chair of the Music4children charity, whose members broke the world record for "The Highest Gig" by performing on Mount Everest in 2012. Jennifer has worked with the international poet Spike Hawkins, editing his book 250 Grams of Poetry, *and formed the theater company Queenie Productions, where she serves as co-director and producer. She is currently helping to set up an organization for transformational entrepreneurs, relaxing as a fitness instructor specializing in working with disabilities and getting back into theater and short filmmaking.*

Chapter 13

Something *Big* Is about to Happen!
Nine Tips for Surviving and
Thriving Despite Challenges

Ronica Arnold Branson

Y ou know the feeling when there's about to be a change in your life? That inner voice that tells you something *big* is about to happen? I've had that feeling before and I'm having it again right now. Something big is about to happen in my life, something positive, and now, as you read, I hope something big might be about to happen in your life, too!

Not long ago, I made the decision to start sharing my experience of life with others. This hasn't been an easy decision for me; in fact, it's something I've struggled with for many years. You see, I'm a very private person, and I've made a concerted effort to keep things to myself and deal with my issues on my own. But, at this point in my life, I feel it's time to change. It's time to heal, time to share and, hopefully, time to turn my hurt into someone else's healing.

Why have I waited? For one thing, I have to talk about a disease I have that's embarrassing to me: inflammatory bowel disease (IBD). Yes, I know, "everyone poops," but still… When you have IBD, because of the inflammation you tend to poop more than others and often at the most inconvenient times. So, I've lived with emotional challenges, as well as the challenges of daily pain, fatigue and scary life-changing experiences.

IBD is an "invisible illness." You look fine on the outside, so it can be hard for people to understand that you aren't fine on the inside. With the exception of the weight I've lost and gained because of treatments and illness, it doesn't look like there's anything wrong with me at all—though the medical reports tell a very different story. Also, I do a good job of hiding the pain, both physically and emotionally. I've lived by the motto "Never let them see you sweat" and tried to keep smiling despite the pain. I've minimized my illness because I know many people have much greater limitations.

On the upside, I am continually reminded not to take the little things for granted. Although I have my challenges, I feel touched every time I see someone with what I call a differing ability. It takes a strong person to carry on in life when you live with a uniqueness that many people may never understand. It also helps to know that I am not alone with my physical challenges.

Recently, I saw a young man who was differently abled. He walked with a limp and his limbs weren't straight, and my heart was immediately touched. I wondered what life might be like for him. Did it hurt for him to walk? How did he feel about the stares he received from people? How did his mom and his family handle all the emotions of having a child with a unique appearance and ability?

I could empathize with them because, some years ago, my brother LA sustained very serious injuries as a result of being in a car accident. During the accident his car slid under a truck, and he suffered a massive head injury. The doctors did emergency surgery on him that night, and we all prayed that God would just let him live, and God did just that. LA lived, but he no longer had the capacity to walk, talk or do anything for himself.

When my family and I would take LA to appointments and other public places, people would stare. I was very protective of him and didn't like the stares. Even though LA couldn't express himself, I'm sure deep down he didn't like them either. It was so hard for my parents and me, but I know it was even harder for him. The doctors recommended that we institutionalize LA, but that was a no-go for us. Home was where he was supposed to be. We never knew how much he remembered, or if he even knew who we were, but we showed him our love, and hopefully that made things a little bit more bearable for him.

The doctors said that LA would never show emotion and would always be in a coma-like state, but that wasn't the case. He did smile and laugh, and he also cried. Sometimes when we'd walk in the room he'd have the biggest smile, but toward the end, he just turned away. He didn't really want to eat or even watch his favorite TV shows.

LA lived for nine years after the accident. I knew it was inevitable, but it was still very hard for me when he died. I always prayed for a miracle healing, but his miracle healing came when he was released from his earthly pain.

Throughout LA's struggle I was having my own health challenges with the chronic IBD, and, after he passed, a new diagnosis seemed to be added to my chart each time I went to the doctor. First, I was diagnosed with a (supposedly) terminal illness, ovarian cancer, and had a large mass removed and a liver and kidney transplant. Then I had an aneurysm as a complication that stemmed from repairing three blockages in my heart and then emergency surgery to repair that. Next came another myocardial infarction that I didn't find out about until days later. I had multiple hospitalizations and way too many doctor's visits and trips to the emergency room to count.

At one point I asked myself, *Is it worth it to keep going?* But luckily I didn't let that question rule my life. I had to know that all of this was for a much greater purpose. Deep down I believed that there was a gift hidden somewhere in the suffering.

Today, I know that the gift is the fact that I now live each day knowing that I am very blessed to still be here! There are days when I can't believe that *I am still standing*. As my friends say, the Bionic Woman has nothing on me!

So, something *big* did happen in my life. I know that medical science saved me, but there were so many lucky breaks and fortunate coincidences that the only way I can explain my survival is to tell you that I have been divinely blessed and highly favored. I am nothing but a walking, talking, breathing miracle!

Feeling so grateful, I asked myself the question: *How could I not share my story?* This kind of stuff doesn't just happen for no reason! I believe that my life is a testament that we can learn and grow from our hardships. So I started trying to write my story, but it was like pulling teeth from a cat! If you've seen the movie *The Help*, you'll remember the powerful scenes in which Viola Davis's character talks with the little girl and tells her, "You is kind… you is smart… you is important." Well, that's what I had to keep on telling myself: "You are smart… you are creative… you can do this!" It's been hard to get it down on paper, but I know that doing so will change my life in unknown, wonderful ways.

I'm so happy to be able to share with you the following "healing helpers" that have guided me along my journey. If you can live by them, I know you'll see something *big* happen for you, too!

Healing Helper #1: Practice Gratitude

> *"If the only prayer you said was 'Thank you,' that would be enough."*
> **—Meister Eckhart**

What do you have to be thankful for? If nothing else, give thanks for today, because no matter what you are facing, you are still here. Be thankful that today you have the strength to walk on your own, to express yourself and to have the opportunity to see another beautiful day. Life is not going to be perfect, but we must remain optimistic and know that tomorrow is a brand-new day and a brand-new chance to make a change. Be thankful for today and look forward to brighter tomorrows. I know that things get hard. Even if you aren't experiencing any difficulties right now, you can simply turn on the news and see all the madness that's taking place in our world. But being grateful for the good in your life will help make things better.

Healing Helper #2: Have Faith

> *"Faith is the substance of things hoped for,*
> *the evidence of things not yet seen."*
> **—Matthew 17:20**

We were never promised that life would be easy. Yes, things do get hard. As Langston Hughes put it, "Life for me ain't been no crystal stair." When you feel you don't have any more to give, keep on fighting and keep believing that things will get better. Don't give up. Don't give in. Although you can't see the outcome, you have to envision the victory. Just like you have faith that you can get on a plane and trust that it will take you to your destination. Have the same type of faith in knowing that things will get better.

Healing Helper #3: Be Willing to Forgive

"Forgiveness is not an occasional act, it is a constant attitude."
—Martin Luther King Jr.

Forgive yourself and others. What if every day when we woke up we were reminded of our past faults and our transgressions? We would be in pretty bad shape. So, with the same thought, we must recognize that we can't constantly relive the wrongs of others or ourselves. Forgive those who have wronged you, but first forgive yourself. It will help you in more ways than one. When you use the magic of forgiveness, so many positive things will start to manifest in your life, and so much weight will be lifted. You may even begin to feel like a new person. So, why not give it a try?

Healing Helper #4: Appreciate Your Family, Friends, Caregivers and Support System

"When we demonstrate our appreciation for the support we receive from others, it reinforces that behavior and deepens our connection to them."
—Marci Shimoff

They didn't have to do the things they did. They don't have to be there with you now to support you. Appreciate that they are. Too often we forget to show appreciation to those who have done the most for us. A simple word, a call, a smile or a hug—just to say, *I appreciate you*—can make a difference in a person's life. Thank your family for loving you—and forget about their imperfections. Thank your doctors for treating you. Thank your children for bringing joy into your life. But don't stop there. Show random acts of kindness to those you appreciate, and they'll appreciate *you* even more for it.

Healing Helper #5: Practice Positive Thinking

"Life is 10 percent what you make it and 90 percent how you take it."
—**Irving Berlin**

Time and time again, it has been proven that a positive thought, word or action can be the difference between a positive or negative outcome. Waking up on the wrong side of the bed every day with a bad attitude will get you just what you expect: a bad day! On the other hand, waking up with a positive attitude and speaking affirmations, such as "Today is going to be an *awesome* day" or "Today is the start of something beautiful," can't help but give you a happier state of mind and a more successful way of life.

Healing Helper #6: Live, Laugh, Love…Today!

"Never put off till tomorrow what you can do today."
—**Thomas Jefferson**

What if tomorrow was your last day? Would you have regrets? Would you wish you had lived more, laughed more, loved more? It's not too late! Start today. Life is for the living. Enjoy the things that you can enjoy—the beautiful flowers, the ability to dance to your favorite music. Heck, when was the last time you danced in the rain? If you have never tried it, you're missing out on something big. Don't take life so seriously! Laughter can be the greatest medicine and just what you need to heal your soul.

And you can't let life go by without giving and receiving love. It is one of the greatest gifts we have been given. Just because you have been hurt once, don't shortchange yourself. You deserve to be loved. Don't wait for it to find you: go out there and get it!

Healing Helper #7: Know that "This Too Shall Pass" and Pain Is Not Permanent

> *"You never know how strong you are*
> *until being strong is the only choice you have."*
> **—Bob Marley**

Although you may be hurting right now, know that it is only temporary. I define hurt as a Horrible Unfair Reality that is only Temporary. It's kind of like hitting your toe; it hurts terribly when it happens, but the pain eventually subsides. Whatever you are facing today, know that the pain of the situation will not last forever. Day by day, step by step, it will get better. You may not be able to see the sunshine beyond the clouds, but know that it is there. Your sunshine is coming, if it's not already there, right in front of your face!

Healing Helper #8: Have Courage

> *"Courage isn't having the strength to go on.*
> *It is going on when you don't have strength."*
> **—Napoleon**

There comes a time when you must step out in faith and fight fear, if only to save your own life. Courage is simply faith in action. You don't know how you're going to do it, but in order to get to the next step, in order to heal, in order to live your destiny, you are going to have to do some things that you are afraid to do. Whether it's quitting that job that's causing you so much stress it's making you sick, or having that surgery you know you need in order to live a better life, you have to do it. And even if it's going up to that person who wronged you and saying "I forgive you" without expecting anything in return, you can do it. You have all the courage you need to win the battle.

Healing Helper #9: Surrender to Life

> *"Surrender to what is. Say 'yes' to life—and see how*
> *life suddenly starts working for you rather than against you."*
> **—Eckhart Tolle**

Yes, here's some advice that may not be what you're expecting: at some point, you may have to surrender. There may be a time when you will just need to let go and be still. When you've done all you can do, you have to remember that sometimes saying "yes" to what is, is the most powerful thing you can do. Let it go, let God and simply watch the miracle unfold.

No matter what you're going through right now, I urge you to choose to believe in miracles. You may be hurting or healing; you may be in chaos or crisis, or headed there fast. Just remember this: when you change your thoughts, your life changes. Take these nine points and try to live by them. If you can, even a little, I promise you, something *big* will happen!

Ronica Arnold Branson, PhD, is a counselor, coach, inspirational speaker, author and survivor. She knows firsthand what it's like to face crisis situations and, through them, discover the power of faith, prayer and divine intervention. Through resiliency, determination and support from loved ones; through the help of divine spirits that have crossed her path; and, most importantly, through witnessing God perform miracles in her life, she is still here today.

Ronica believes that everyone has the right to a healthy state of being—physically, mentally and spiritually. However, problems in these areas are often neglected in our everyday chaos until we experience a crisis. Grateful for the lessons she's learned, Ronica has dedicated her life to supporting others through their pain and helping them create an awareness of miracles in their lives in any situation. For more information about Ronica, her work and her journey, visit her at www.drronica.com.

———— Chapter 14 ————

When Those You've Counted On Are Counting On You: How to Find Balance When Caring for Aging Parents

Debra Kelsey-Davis

H ow can this be happening?"

"What are we going to do?"

The words swirled round and round in my head. I couldn't make a sound as I choked back my tears. There she was, our mom, on the stretcher, once again being rushed from the nursing home to the emergency room, her pleading eyes seeking ours. And there I stood, helpless and scared.

If you've ever watched one of your parents falter and become vulnerable, you probably know what it feels like. The gut-wrenching emotions. The waves of fear when the tables turn and the parent who's always taken care of you now needs you to care for them. Chances are, the reality is that, if you're blessed to still have a living parent, one day you'll be caring for them—and wondering how you're going to be able to do it. Or maybe you're in the midst of it right now. For me, it's round two in my family-caregiving journey!

I used to think that by the time my parents were old and needed my help I would somehow just know what to do. How's that for being prepared?! Hopefully I've not offended you if that's been your go-to plan, too. Truly, we are not alone. I've learned that very few of us are fully aware of what's really involved in caring for a loved one.

Oh, how I wish I'd been more prepared, but, like so many of us, I was overloaded and barely keeping up with everyday life. Whether you have a family of your own, a demanding job or both, so many things vie for your attention these days. Being a registered nurse, I thought it might easier for me than most—I should have all the preparation I could need, right? Nope! Medical training didn't tell me what I needed to plan for regarding caregiving, or how to cope. Science teaches us much, but not how to care for the soul and *from* the soul.

I want you to have the benefit of lessons and tools I didn't have, whether you're faced with this challenge today or still cruising along with independent parents. But first I'd like to share the story of how this came about for me.

Learning from Eva

My mother-in-law, Eva, wasn't always sick and helpless; "feisty" was a better way to describe her personality. Up to the moment everything changed, she was a vibrant 72-year-old woman who played a mean hand of cards and every day walked her condo's nature path.

What I didn't see coming happened on a hot August day at the family lake home, Eva's favorite place. As was our tradition, my husband's siblings and all our families had converged that summer to enjoy boating and campfires together at Lake Shelbyville before the kids headed back to school.

After kitchen cleanup one morning, we were all sipping our coffee and chatting in the family room, when, without warning, Eva said, "We need to talk."

Quietly she took a deep breath and said, "I have cancer."

Silence. We were shocked.

Wringing her hands, she said, "I don't know what to do."

The questions started coming, and then everyone was talking at the same time:

"What did the doctor say?"

"What kind?"

"Should we go to the University of Chicago Hospital?"

"Who should we talk to?"

"Should we go to Loyola instead?"

"Mom, what do *you* want to do?"

As an in-law, I was reluctant to say much. But Eva had always treated me as a daughter, and I loved her as a mother. So, when she turned to me, the nurse in the room, and asked, "What should I do?" I replied, "I'm not sure. We really need to get more information… for you… for all of us, to really know where to start."

So, we did the research and Eva saw several doctors and we made a plan. Then, just three months into Eva's battle with cancer, after radiation and unsuccessful rounds of chemotherapy, her body began to fail. The doctors suggested she be placed in a nursing home—the last place we wanted to consider. But she was very sick, and we all had full-time jobs and young kids. Ultimately, Eva made the decision to move in to the nursing home.

I was very worried, recalling the negative experiences I'd seen when visiting my grandparents in nursing homes. Yet, I was able to ease my mind by thinking, *We'll get involved. We can tackle it as a team.* With her daughter Nancy being an ultrasound technician, her son-in-law Russ an orthopedic surgeon and me a nurse, clinically, we should have this covered.

I was naïve. We quickly discovered that much more than our clinical experience was needed. First, communication was an issue. The staff didn't want to deal with our questions nor hear our concerns. And we weren't always on the same page. We were stressed. Eva's dignity had been stripped away by the impersonal "care" she barely received. And when the monies from Medicare quickly ran out, we had no good alternative planned, meaning we would have to come up with $9,000 a month to keep her there!

But it turned out to be safety issues that pushed us over the edge. We were shocked to arrive one night to find her naked, tangled in the sheets, hanging partially out of the bed and calling for help, her call light on for God knows how long and no one responding. That was it! We needed to get her out of there. I reduced my hours at work and requested permission to work from home, making it possible to bring her to our home to care for her there.

I'll be honest with you—it wasn't an easy job. I learned a *lot*. I came to see that it was compassion, laughter and loving patience that made the real difference, and not the medical tasks of feeding, medicating and turning. I learned that daily baths with lavender-perfumed scents made her feel more her old self again. It was about honoring her wishes. Sure, I cared for her body—but I also learned how to care for her soul.

This was rewarding, but at the same time I could see the wear and tear of stress on me. I wasn't taking care of my needs, and I knew I absolutely had to start making room for my own fun and rest. Once I did that (and stuck to it!), I found joy in sharing stories with Eva, painting her nails and watching the birds from our back porch. In those few months, our relationship deepened. Her gift to me was the privilege of caring for her.

The Realization

After Eva passed, I went back to my job as a VP in a healthcare management company, but I found I felt empty in that world now. I decided to leave my career and suddenly had a lot of time on my hands. I began reaching out to friends and colleagues I'd not spoken to in ages, and it was very interesting; in nearly every conversation, I heard of the struggles people were having caring for their aging parents. There were stories of trying to care for a parent who had fallen or one whose memory loss could no longer be ignored, and of the challenges of moving a parent into senior housing. So, it wasn't just me who had had to deal with this. I was just now waking up to what seemed like an epidemic. If you and I had talked, would I have heard a similar story from you?

It makes sense. More people are living to ripe old ages, and the sandwich generation, or baby boomers, are hitting the headlines with their own stories and pleas for support.

It dawned on me that maybe I had something unique. I had the experience of actively caring for family (now including my own aging parents), plus years of nursing and working inside the healthcare system to improve overall population health. Could these chapters in my life be a gift I was being called to share?

People kept pushing me to tell my story and pass along what I'd learned. I took that as a sign to move forward.

You Can Meet This Challenge and Find Balance in Your Life

If you're facing the prospect of caring for a parent, my question for you is this: Do you wonder if it's possible to find peace, and even joy, during such a challenging time in your life? Well, imagine for a moment a big event in your life that took a lot of preparation time and confrontation with obstacles. Let's use planning a wedding as an example. Ask yourself:

Did I need help?

Was it stressful dealing with the multitude of wedding tasks?

Did I use a wedding planner (whether a person or notebook)?

Did I assign roles with specific responsibilities?

How much research did I have to do?

Did communications ever get mixed up or family dynamics interfere?

Did I set goals?

Okay, let's fast-forward to the day after the wedding. Despite the stress, the tears and maybe a fight or two leading up to the big day, did you also experience joy and satisfaction much of the time? I hope your answer is the same as mine: "Yes!" It is indeed possible to cope and find contentment under super-stressful situations. You have the ability to find joy amidst the challenges of a supposedly joyous activity like planning a wedding or a supposedly challenging event like caring for an aging parent. But you'll need support. I'd like to share what I've learned, so you'll be ready when the day comes.

A Guide for the Journey

The best advice I *never* received was to prepare early for being a caregiver. And, the second-best advice I *never* received was to diligently care for myself while in the caregiving role. Trust me. Make these your priorities, whether you're thinking of how to prepare or have already embarked on your caregiving journey.

Here are eight more guidelines I've found helpful and hope you will, too:

Guideline #1: Roles

Get clear on roles right up front. Know your role and your responsibilities and those of family members and other helpers. Know who's going to be the durable power of attorney for health and for finances. Confirm who's going to be the primary caregiver. If you're an only child, enlist help from family and friends and bring in professional caregiving help as needed. Decide who's going to arrange for transportation, housework, food shopping, preparing meals, managing finances, communicating with medical personnel, etc. Know what's involved and how it will impact your job, family, finances, health and other commitments. Delegate and make sure roles and expectations are understood. And, take care of *you* by setting boundaries and remembering that the role does not define who you are.

Guideline #2: Communication

It may not always be comfortable, but "having the talks" about responsibilities, expectations, mix-ups, failures and so on is critical. Speak openly, honestly and directly, always. Confront family dynamics. If your family is like mine, personalities and childhood rivalries could cause flare-ups. If necessary, get a neutral third party to intervene. Have family meetings and record decisions, commitments and wishes, and share key information. Centralize communications for everyone to access. And, take care of *you* by having a confidant you can talk things through with and get support from.

Guideline #3: Resources

Learn the landscape and educate yourself. Identify what agencies and people to go to for help, including medical, spiritual, legal and financial resources. Often, not having enough money becomes a source of great worry. Tap into social workers, financial advisors or other helpers who can identify potential sources of aid. And please remember to take care of *you* and join a support group.

Guideline #4: Planning

Know your gaps and create a plan to guide others in sharing responsibilities. Start by assessing needs. For example, do you know where your parents' important papers are, and do you have access to them? Do you understand their finances and the impact of caregiving on your own financial situation? Have you reviewed your parents' medications and created a current, complete list? Do you have a plan for emergencies? Is there an end-of-life plan? Don't forget to take care of *you* and schedule time to rest.

Guideline #5: Safety

Make safety a high priority. Evaluate your parents' home environment. Is there a risk of falls due to throw rugs or uneven stairs? Have you recently ridden in a car driven by your parents, and are they safe to continue to drive? Have you gone through the medicine cabinet together and tossed out all outdated medications? Take care of *you* by checking in weekly on your own physical health, safety and emotional well-being.

Guideline #6: Quality of Life

Focus on their quality of life. Do you know their wishes regarding end-of-life issues? Can their routines be maintained? Help your parents to be seen as real people by the care team, and make their stories known to them. Advocate for them. And take care of *you* by sticking to your routines, too!

Guideline #7: Activities

It's all about remaining active and socially connected. Older adults often love to have regularly scheduled activities so they have something to look forward to each day. Use games and one-on-one time to recall memories. Make sure community ties to places like church and clubs are maintained. Take care of *you* by carving time out for respite and engaging in activities you enjoy.

Guideline #8: Preservation

Capture their life stories to create a legacy. Collect memories. Create digital storybooks. Interview them and collect stories about them from others who've known them over the years. Take care of *you* by keeping a journal and meditating.

Take 15 minutes now to quickly get a sense of how prepared you are in each of these eight areas. If you see gaps, don't worry; I had gaping holes at first. You will get there! My biggest problem was overcoming my pride and asking others for help. Surround yourself with a team and, together, work through each of these eight areas, one by one. Keep track so you can see your progress, and it will seem less overwhelming. And don't be surprised when you need to go back and make changes. Life is constantly changing as circumstances change, right?

I revisit and reassess each of these areas at least once a month with my family, and together we make adjustments. Remember, you can minimize the stress, the fear and the helpless feelings by preparing and following through in these eight areas. That leaves more room for creating memories, for finding joy in the time you have together and for achieving balance in your own life And when the time comes, you'll be able to let go of your mom or dad with the deep fulfillment of knowing that, when they needed you most, you were there.

 *After 35 years as a clinician and respected healthcare executive, Deb Kelsey-Davis left corporate America to serve families caring for aging parents. Dismayed by appalling encounters with today's broken care system, Deb is determined to improve the quality of life of family caregivers and of those for whom they care.*

With deep compassion, Deb writes and speaks on the caregiving journey, based on caring for her mother-in-law and her parents. In 2015, she launched Soul-to-Soul Solutions, with a faith-based program and workshop series for caregivers, knowing just how frequently caregivers find themselves at the crossroads of faith, fear, frustration and loneliness.

In her book, The Ruby Slippers Principle, *Deb provides emotional support and powerful insights, plus effective tools and provocative answers to discovering what really matters when coping with one of life's most difficult yet rewarding transitions.*

To contact Deb for speaking, workshops or coaching services, visit her at www.S2S.Care.

Chapter 15

From Broken to Beautiful:
Five Steps to Transform Your Life

Jeanette Jardine

Humpty Dumpty sat on a wall,
Humpty Dumpty had a great fall.
All the king's horses and all the king's men
Couldn't put Humpty together again.

I was Humpty Dumpty. I felt broken. I had cracked wide open and was in a thousand tiny pieces.

We had looked like the perfect family—we even lived in a big white house on a hill. My four children were handsome and beautiful and successful in school and sports, as well as socially. My husband was tall, dark and, yes, handsome, and he had the best sense of humor of anyone I have ever known. But there were many challenges, and, to make a very long story very short, I ultimately filed for and obtained a divorce, after a lengthy, bitter and exhausting battle.

And then I broke into many little pieces, just like Humpty Dumpty.

Don't get me wrong: I was glad to be divorced. And, on a deep level, I was also glad that the last child was off to college and all four were doing exceptionally well. But, sitting in the house all alone, I experienced a very personal collapse. My whole purpose in living was suddenly gone, along with my whole way of life. I had no idea where to go from here. Who was I? The trauma of our final years together and the divorce process had squashed my self-image and drained me of the strength I needed in order to create a new life.

I knew I had to figure out a way to heal, and I made myself work hard at it. For months I went to therapists, psychics, acupuncturists, spiritual healers and shamans—so many that I began to lose track of who was who. Plus, I read every self-help book I could get my hands on. Yet, as time passed, it didn't seem to be working. I still felt shattered in body, mind and spirit.

And then one day, months later, as I sat slumped on the sofa, suddenly everything changed. Through the grace of God, all the knowledge I had been absorbing clicked and I had a deep realization: *only I could heal me*. No one else could do it. I had made the choices I had made, and I had to put the pieces back together *myself*.

With that thought came a sudden flood of others, so I jumped up and sat down at my computer. I opened a new document and typed the letters "STARR." They just came to me. And then I typed:

Surrender to what is.

Trust in my destiny.

Accept today with gratitude.

Release my past.

Receive all the goodness surely coming my way.

This acronym and its meaning came as a gift to me, and I have repeated it to myself countless times every day and night for the past four years. It's no exaggeration to say that it saved my life.

One definition of the word "star" is "a conventional or stylized representation of a star, typically one having five or more points." My STARR has five points and, like a star, it has been a light that has led me through the dark years of my recovery and healing from years of trauma. I had thought that I was Humpty Dumpty, but soon I realized I knew something Humpty Dumpty did *not* know. This is my poem now:

> Sad little Jeanette sat on a wall.
> Sad little Jeanette had a great fall.
> All of her family and all of her friends
> Couldn't put Jeanette together again.
> *Jeanette* put Jeanette together again.

If my STARR worked for me, it can work for you, too. Each of my STARR's five points has helped me to find the healing and peace I was searching for. Let me begin with the first. There is a rhyme and reason to the order of each point; they are the sequential steps we have to take to heal ourselves.

Point #1: Surrender to What Is

Surrender is the first and top point of my STARR. Like Maslow's hierarchy of needs, my STARR has a beginning point and an end point. This was my place to start the healing process.

Surrender is a tough one. It's really, really hard to do, but it's possible—and essential. Say to yourself, out loud, "I surrender to **what is.**" In other words, I will not fight or resist my present situation. "What you resist, persists," Carl Jung said. So, if you don't like the situation you're in, surrendering your resistance to it is the first step to ending it.

For me, surrender looked like this: *Okay, I spent the first half of my life the way I did, and now I have to find a totally different life to live. The past is the past! I will not fight those old fights anymore. I am here now, with these strengths and these weaknesses. This is what is, and I accept it as God's gift to me!*

By surrendering, you stop fighting a losing battle. When you stop resisting and see your situation clearly, *just as it is,* things begin to change. Your resistance is your natural protective mechanism to guard yourself from pain. But when you can say, "This is the truth about my life right now," you let go of this shield and allow yourself to be present in your life, just as you are right now. This can be very painful or it can be a relief. But, either way, it's the necessary first step to making a change.

It's not easy to surrender and accept what is, but when you realize that you can't stop hurting until you do, you can find the strength to do it.

Point #2: Trust in My Destiny

Trust is another difficult assignment, especially when you have lost faith in yourself. I had lost all confidence in my ability to make healthy decisions. After all, hadn't I stayed in a difficult situation for many years? How could I have let that happen? Well, it was my choice, but I can always make different choices.

Say these words, out loud: "I trust myself and my destiny." Repeat these words often, and allow yourself to listen to your own inner feelings. When you choose to trust in your ability to listen to your authentic self and follow your destiny, you open yourself up to new possibilities. You "unstick" yourself from your old story.

"No trumpets sound when the important decisions of our life are made. Destiny is made known silently," said Agnes de Mille. Your destiny is unfolding with every choice you make. As you learn to trust your destiny and yourself, you discover that you can create a beautiful life if you are true to yourself at every crossroad and always follow your highest principles, your intuition and your heart. As Shakespeare said, "To thine own self be true."

Point #3: Accept Today with Gratitude

Here's another challenge that seems impossible at first. But say these words out loud anyway: "I accept today with gratitude." Gratitude is huge! According to Cicero, "Gratitude is not only the greatest of virtues but the parent of all others." It's essential to your recovery process. My life changed the minute I could accept my circumstances and feel grateful for the blessings I had *in this moment*, instead of drowning in resentment and bitterness over wrongs done to me in the past.

Physicists tell us our thoughts become things—for good or ill. And your thoughts are your choice! So, begin by thanking God, even if all you can appreciate right now is that you are vertical!

Accepting each day with gratitude will change more than your attitude: it will change your circumstances. As you improve your inner reality, your outer reality will inevitably improve, too. And acceptance includes accepting yourself for exactly who you are, with gratitude for the gifts you're blessed with (and we're all blessed with some!) and also for the challenges that have made you stronger.

Point #4: Release My Past

Sometimes it's very hard to let your past go—but it's never impossible. Say it out loud: "I release my past." Or you might prefer "I release my pain." Saying it helps to make it happen. I had to work very hard on this because I had become almost obsessed with my past and the pain that lingered from it. Looking back, I can see that I was, in a way, addicted to telling the story of my grievances over and over—and that wasn't doing me or anyone any good.

The commitment to let go of your painful past will catapult you to freedom. Your determination to let go of your old story will liberate you not only from a lot of pain but from many false beliefs you have unconsciously held.

Have you been beating yourself up for the actions and choices that got you where you are today? A healthier choice is to shift your thinking to: "That was then." Forgive yourself and resolve to be wiser going forward. We all have our story. What I decided was that, though my past had shaped the woman I had become, I would not allow it to define my future. I was worthy of much more than the story I had lived the last 29 years. By releasing the painful story of those years, I reclaimed myself. I took back my power and my authentic self.

I wanted desperately to heal and to release the toxic emotions of the past so they wouldn't fester inside of me. But I realized these emotions couldn't be released and healed until I loved and forgave myself. So I made the decision that I would treat myself the way I wanted others to treat me. This included having compassion for myself and treating myself with kindness. This changed everything—but I couldn't do it until I released the past.

Point #5: Receive All the Goodness Surely Coming My Way

For many of us, this last point of the STARR is an enormous challenge. Some might scratch their heads and say, "Why would it be difficult to receive? Especially the good stuff!" But if you know what I'm talking about, say out loud: "I receive all the goodness that is my birthright and is right in front of me." It may have been harder to do this than you think!

I still struggle with this one. Sometimes I still catch myself dwelling on hurts from the past and suffering all over again, instead of enjoying a pleasure that's right in front of me! It's like a strange addiction to feeling the pain of the old wounds, and an avoidance of happiness. And that happens to many, if not most, of us. Of course we all want to receive love and abundance and peace and health and happiness. But, for those of us who have experienced trauma, it can be almost impossible to believe in goodness and open our hearts to it. We're terrified because of the hurt we experienced when we did that in the past. After that, it can be almost impossible to have the courage to put all that behind us and open ourselves up and become vulnerable once more.

But again I say, "What are our options?" Do we want to be alone forever? Distrustful of life? Or do we want to be open to what might come?" I did not want to live the rest of my life "walking safely on the sidewalk," as Kelly Clarkson sings.

This point is about letting go of your armor, your defenses and your fear, and opening up your heart and letting yourself feel the joy of being alive. Once you choose to receive with an open heart, you step into new territory where you are graced with access to your divine nature. This is a necessary step if you want to choose the kind of person you want to be. I knew I did not want to live a small life; I wanted to use my power to manifest the life of my dreams.

"If there be a faith that can move mountains, it is faith in one's own power," said Marie von Ebner-Eschenbach. As I grew in that power, I could open up and receive what God and the universe were offering me. It was mine to take—and enjoy.

We can each follow our own STARR and take the time to really "talk the talk and walk the walk." If you can stay with it, you'll be amazed by your healing process. Healing is much like grief: it's a uniquely personal journey. There are no rules and no timetables. I know it's hard to have the patience to take the time it takes. Believe me, I've been very impatient with my own healing. For me, it's taken over four years, for goodness' sake! (Or you could even say it's taken my whole life.) I have too often snapped at myself, "Jeanette, what is wrong with you?!"

Now I get it—and you can, too. Just be gentle with yourself, my friend. Forgive yourself. Treat yourself the way you would treat someone you dearly loved. Set your intention to heal, and then attend to that intention. Each day do what you can to reach that goal, and then let it go at the end of each day. You did your best—and your best may not be much some days. But tomorrow is another day. As the quote from Mary Anne Radmacher on my refrigerator says: "Courage does not always roar. Sometimes courage is the quiet voice at the end of the day saying, 'I will try again tomorrow.'"

And one more thing: don't believe everything you read—including old nursery rhymes! Humpty Dumpty didn't know about this five-pointed STARR approach to healing. If he had, he wouldn't have needed all the king's horses and all the king's men to put him together again. Humpty could have drawn on all the wisdom he had gained on his journey and done it all on his own!

Jeanette Jardine lived in New England for 30 years while raising her four children, who are now thriving adults. Since her divorce she has been on a quest for her own spiritual growth, and she continues each day to embrace her inner light and hard-won self-love. She enjoys traveling, running, volunteering with charitable groups and reading. Currently, Jeanette is writing her first book. Her intention is to help others who have experienced trauma to find their path to a full healing. She hopes to inspire many to break out of unfulfilling circumstances and rediscover how wonderful life can be.

---------------- *Chapter 16* ----------------

What to Do When Your Life
is Being Turned Upside Down
Linda Solberg

"Mommy, my feet hurt," my four-year-old daughter said.

Lisa's heels were hurting again, this time so badly that she wasn't able to stand. This was one of several symptoms she'd been experiencing for the past few months. I knew the pain would only last a few minutes because her father had had this symptom for a period in his life. Eventually Gustav was diagnosed with Lyme disease. He and I were both upset at the prospect that Lisa might also have Lyme—it had proven to be a long, hard, ongoing struggle for him.

Little did I dream that these symptoms would lead to almost losing custody of my child. What follows was one of the most challenging times of my life, but I came out of it realizing that what seemed to be a punishment in my life was actually a great gift. In sharing my story and the lessons I learned from this heart-wrenching experience, I hope you'll discover your own gifts by using the tools I provide to face your challenges with love and self-compassion.

Gustav and I were separated when Lisa complained about her feet hurting, and he lived five hours away, near Oslo, the capital of Norway, so we talked by phone.

"There has to be someone out there who can help us," I said, thinking of all the ignorance we had run into when he had become ill.

"Well, just don't tell any new doctor that I've got Lyme," Gustav said. "They'll just think you're a hypochondriac." He was currently receiving medical treatments from a doctor he had found in Germany.

A part of me agreed. When Gustav fell ill, our public health system had refused to diagnose him with Lyme disease, saying multiple sclerosis was the right diagnosis. They simply didn't believe Lyme disease was a real ailment. But another part of me wanted to think differently. Hopefully, things had improved, four years later. I thought, *If I can tell the truth to a new doctor, maybe Lisa can get some help.*

So, I had hope when we got an appointment with a young female doctor in the Norwegian healthcare system, whom I'll call Dr. Perenni. My hopes were dashed, though, when Dr. Perenni got upset as soon as I mentioned that, based on Lisa's father's similar symptoms, we thought it was Lyme disease. She interrupted me repeatedly, and I got so annoyed that I started to interrupt her. When I mentioned the bacteria called Bartonella, which is known as a co-infection to Lyme, she said she'd never heard of it. Then she seemed to feel threatened by me and got even colder.

I had never argued with a doctor before, but this time I'd had enough. When Dr. Perenni said the time was up, I told her I'd find a private doctor to help us if she wasn't willing. She looked at Lisa with a sad expression, then turned to me and said, "You know, it's really important not to make one's child ill by focusing on symptoms of all kinds. Also, you shouldn't believe everything you read on the Internet." Her belief that Lyme was a myth overrode all our long-term experience.

When we left her office, I thought we were done, but, to my surprise, Dr. Perenni called a week later and told me how worried she'd been. "I've been thinking a lot about you and Lisa," she said. "Why would you want to go to a private clinic? Norway has the best public health system in the world."

When I told Dr. Perenni my reasons, and she realized that I wouldn't go any further with the public system, she announced that she had to turn me in to the Child Protection Services (CPS). This was chilling news to me. The Norwegian Child Protection Services is not known for its loving approach to families. They act as if they are placed above the law, so at this point I felt defeated before the game was even on.

I was also worn out from struggling with other problems, in addition to Lisa's health issues. Gustav's health worried me, and I was exhausted from being a single mom for four years. I was studying to become a teacher at the time and had lots of books to read and presentations to write and deliver—and I was so tired I could hardly think. It was a hard time to be facing such a serious problem.

When I told the staff at Lisa's kindergarten about my experience with the new doctor, they seemed to get upset on my behalf.

"We'd like to support you," the director said, "but the only way we can do that and attend the meetings with Child Protection Services is if we turn you in, too."

At this point I was confused and in total despair. But I knew I needed some support, and I felt they were being honest about their willingness to help, so I reluctantly agreed to their doing that.

In the coming weeks, staff from the CPS made several visits to our home and also had days of observation in the kindergarten. At this time, I was writing my bachelor's degree and preparing for two big exams. I felt my whole life had turned into a war zone, where my main focus had to be on survival. The people at CPS were sure I was doing something wrong in my relationship with Lisa, and they seemed irritated when they couldn't find anything. They took the notice from the doctor very seriously, and I could feel their determination to find evidence that the doctor was right.

Ultimately, they concluded that my interaction with my child was great, but I wasn't good at putting up boundaries—I was too kind. Also, they found it very concerning that I had experienced struggles in my own childhood. I was shocked to learn that that was actually reason enough for them to take my child away from me and put her into a foster home.

And then I got a message saying that they would let me know if they decided to do that!

I felt like my world was caving in. I began to have insomnia, anxiety attacks, migraine headaches and nausea on a daily basis. In my heart, I knew I had been a good mother, but they were making me less able to be one. The staff at the kindergarten wanted to help me, but they were never asked to participate in the meetings, as CPS thought their investigator's written report was sufficient.

Over the following months, waiting for their decision, I lost all confidence in myself. I kept going through my own mental list of all the things that were wrong with me. Maybe I was such a bad person that the best thing for Lisa would be to live with another family. Maybe I was mentally ill, as one of the staff at Child Protection Services had suggested in her notes. Maybe the doctor was right and I was the one making my daughter sick. Looking back, I'm terrified to see how close I came to giving up my daughter to authorities who were claiming they knew all about me after sitting on my couch for a few hours and reading two written notices about me.

And then, finally, the ruling came down: I could keep Lisa, and the case was closed. Wow, it was over! They couldn't find signs of neglect, but I did have to attend what they called

"aid measures" because I was giving my daughter "too much of the good stuff."

I was relieved by the verdict but debilitated by the long nightmare I'd been through. I knew I needed some assistance to get on with my life, so I found a wonderful therapist, aptly named Grace, who helped me make some profound changes. My trauma therapy sessions with Grace enabled me to take major steps forward right away. They strengthened my sense of self-worth, increased my inner power and enabled my real identity to come forth.

I also learned a great deal from the way Grace conducted herself. Even the way she greeted me when I arrived was a healing experience. I felt that she could see all the great things in me that others hadn't. In my sessions with Grace, I found myself immersed in compassion, and soon I was able to feel some compassion for myself, too.

Truly, I feel the fact that someone finally saw the goodness in me saved my life. The professionals at CPS and Dr. Perenni hadn't. They seemed to be obsessed with finding everything that was wrong with me. But looking back, I've realized that focusing on all my faults is what *I* had been obsessed with myself. The devastating experience with Child Protection Services was only the outer manifestation of my longtime lack of self-love.

So, over time, I came to see a crazy truth: I have to thank them. My worst enemies, those whom I had raged against, were the ones who ultimately gave me the greatest gift: the realization that I had to look within myself and do some serious healing work to stop hating and start loving myself.

I'm forever grateful to Grace, and also to Janet Attwood, a more recent guide, who helped me let go of the last bits of bitterness about everything that happened to me. With Janet's help, I even let go of my rage toward Dr. Perenni, who had accused me of making my child sick with my beliefs. As Janet said, those bitter feelings would cause severe damage to my mind and body in the long term, so why not be kind to myself and let them go now?

As I've healed, Lisa has also been doing better, although she's still dealing with some health issues. She still hasn't been tested for Lyme disease or any of the common co-infections, as the tests available for this in Norway aren't reliable. I hope we will find the right doctor for her in the near future, and I have a strong feeling it might be an American doctor.

Here are five tools that will make your life better when it's being turned upside down:

Tool #1: Sing the Mantra HU During Times of Hardship

HU (pronounced like the word "hue") is said to be the sound of all the sounds in the universe. It uplifts and soothes the spirit. You can "sing" HU regardless of your beliefs or religion. You do it simply by chanting the mantra over and over, stretching out the syllable in a long, drawn-out sound: HU-U-U-U. Sit in a comfortable position, close your eyes and sing HU for some minutes, and see if you notice feelings of peace, warmth and comfort.

Tool #2: Accept Reality

In the first phase of a traumatic experience, it's natural to go into shock and think, *This cannot be happening.* Then your brain starts to make up a story of what you *think* happened and what you should have done differently to prevent it. This creates a constant conflict in your mind that consumes a lot of energy while not supporting your mental or physical health.

If, instead, you're willing to see things as they really are, you open yourself up to truth. And when truth enters your life, deep healing can take place. Note too that one way to handle the unpleasant feelings you're facing in the process of acceptance is to write down what's going on with you.

Tool #3: Stop Running Away

Running away from ourselves manifests in patterns of excess in our lives, such as going from one relationship to another, working all the time or spending too much time on social media. Notice if you're doing anything to excess and make a commitment to cut back on that activity.

After the incident with Child Protection Services, I was so exhausted I couldn't run away anymore. I was forced to stop and let there be a void in my life. At first, to my great concern, the void filled itself with fear, anxiety and hopelessness. All I could do was breathe and sing HU—but this carried me through. I began to accept that this was how fragile and vulnerable I was. My perception of other people shifted, as I saw that this is how fragile and vulnerable we all are. With this realization, a lot of my anger was replaced by a growing feeling of compassion, both for myself and for others.

Tool #4: Deal With the Internalization of Anger

Loss, or the threat of loss, can stir up a lot of anger and provoke hostile actions toward others. When I was dealing with the CPS, I was yelling at the few important people in my life who were trying to support me, including my mother. I'm still very sorry for not dealing with my anger in a different way. Like so many of us, I wasn't allowed to express anger as a child, so I did what is common: I directed my anger toward myself. I internalized it. When we do that, our anger can become like a ticking bomb that might explode at any time and harm us and those around us.

To undo or prevent this, we can release our internalized anger in many ways. We can "write it out," or paint, run, dance or breathe it out, or scream our anger into some pillows. The important thing is to move the anger out of your body while you still have some control. This greatly empowers you, without harming anyone else.

Tool #5: Get Clarity About Your Values and Commit to Them

Getting clear about your values will help you keep a firm perspective when your life is turned upside down. The main question to ask yourself after hitting rock bottom is this: Do I live my life in accordance with my values? If not, make a commitment to do so. Make a list of five values that are important to you, and choose the two most valuable ones to be your guiding stars in life.

When you are standing at a crossroads in your life and need to make big decisions, remember to check whether your decisions are in accordance with your values or not. Will they bring you closer to or further away from your values?

When you accept the fact that there are things in life that you cannot control, it is easier to be kind to yourself. By committing to your values, you also acknowledge that you are worthy of love and belonging, and that you are willing to co-create your life with a higher source.

Today, I know what I want more of in my life and what I want less of. I know what my values are and what I stand for. I hope that hearing about my experience can help you get to that place in your own life.

Linda Solberg is a mom, teacher and writer who lives in Norway. She is committed to live her life in accordance with her values, which include living with compassion and consideration for future generations. Linda practices self-compassion on a daily basis, hoping to bring more kindness into her life and eventually into the world. You can reach Linda at www.lindasolberg.com.

Chapter 17

The Spirit Process:
11 Gifts from Heaven to Live a Life of Divine Love
Pia Nissen Tylak

W hat was wrong?

From the outside, everything seemed perfect: I was the mother of two wonderful daughters who glowed with happiness, and my long-term boyfriend loved me very much. We had all just moved into our dream house in the country. I was a sought-after transformational speaker and the owner of a large enterprise staffed with 120 creative people. My calendar was full of television jobs lined up for me, and I was financially secure.

But at the very same time, I had never felt more disconnected from my soul. Even as the successes mounted up, it became equally clear to me that I had lost myself in the process. Through the years, I had helped thousands of people live the music of their heart and soul—the very special music we have each been born to create. The problem was, I could no longer remember how to play my own music or walk my own truth. Everywhere I looked, the paths were empty, and

I had no idea how to find the sacred space of love and healing I had once been immersed in.

I felt so ungrateful! How could I, who had achieved so much, not be happy and satisfied? I wondered, *Will I ever feel satisfied?* And then I discovered that another journey was waiting for me. As I share my story, I hope you'll find in it the seeds to discover your path to that sacred space of love that's open to all of us.

The Day I Died

The day began as any other day. The girls and I enjoyed a cozy breakfast, and then off we went to the kindergarten. Everything seemed to be going as usual, but deep inside me I sensed that something was amiss. I tried to shake it off, but just as I kissed my daughters good-bye, I felt a much stronger "farewell" fill my heart. I had the strongest sensation that this would be the last time I would see them.

Suddenly, my heart was beating like crazy, and I knew it was up to me to figure out whether this was a passing fear or another of the premonitions I'd been having since birth. I debated within myself for a while and then decided to go off to work as I had planned. I knew I had to take control of my fear.

At work, one meeting merged into the next, and it was late before I decided it was time to go home. As I drove home, lightning lit up the sky as a thunderstorm ravaged the countryside. And then, all at once, everything changed.

I got a foul taste in my mouth. It almost seemed as if the fillings in my teeth were giving off this taste. I felt a sudden urge to throw up. My fingers went all prickly, like they were being pierced by needles. I went into a cold sweat and clearly sensed that the blood was draining away from my brain. I was so scared.

A pain spread across my chest, and a heavy pressure slowly but surely blocked my airways. I started to gasp for air and blindly jerked the steering wheel to force the car off onto the roadside and brake. At that moment, I went blind.

A sudden coldness wrapped around me. No words. No sounds. Suddenly, as if from a place high up, I saw my self sitting inside the car, seeming to be asleep. All pain disappeared. It felt like I had dismantled my soul. Was I dead?

I thought, *Is this my punishment for never forgiving my father?*

In this uncertain moment, I prayed, with a sincere and fervent heart, that I would be allowed to stay alive. It was unclear to me whether words were rambling out of my mouth or if it was just a jumble of thoughts in my mind.

Suddenly, to the left of me, I saw my two daughters, my sister and my mother. They looked happy and they called out to me. I felt an immense gratitude and wanted to go to them, but then suddenly I saw the most beautiful and divine light to my right side. A hand waved to me from the light, as if it were inviting me to follow it. Never in my life have I felt so drawn to something. With all my soul, I sensed how magnificent it would be to become one with that light. I had no doubt that I was looking into a realm where all my dreams would come true.

I moved toward the realm of light and was just about to enter it, when suddenly I saw blurry words in the air in front of me. They got clearer, and I saw that there were 11 numbered sentences appearing in front of me. I was very irritated by this sight, and in my mind I tried to wave it away. But the words just came closer and closer.

And then, suddenly, I was overwhelmed by an intense feeling of love and compassion, as if every cell in my body was filling up with love, and I knew that I had to take those words seriously. So I focused and read them, and as I understood what they were, I was overwhelmed with gratitude. It was the most beautiful gift from the other side: 11 gifts of wisdom that would change my life and have the power to change anyone's life, forever. I knew right away I had to *live* those 11 gifts to learn how to truly love myself and to be able to help people around the world do the same. I knew they were the key to unblocking our souls' greater purpose and to living a life of supreme love.

As this divine experience slowly faded and I gradually returned to "normal" awareness, I was overwhelmed with emotion, and I felt deeply thankful. I knew now what life wanted from me. I went to the hospital to see what had happened to my body, and the doctor said that I clearly had had a near-death experience and that there was a reason for my return. I knew that reason was the 11 gifts I had been given to share: how to live your Love, Courage, Secrets, Highest Vibration, Tribe, Inner Seer, Inner Child, Wealth, Magic, Silence and Freedom.

I wanted to share them right away, but something was stopping me; I didn't know what. Time passed, and a few years later, I met Dr. Wayne Dyer at an event and we had a private moment to talk. I told him about my experience and the 11 gifts, and he looked deep in my eyes and said, "Pia, please write a book. I want to know every detail. But tell me first, who is the person you need to forgive?"

He was spot on. I had not mentioned my father to Wayne, but I knew, when I heard those words, that before I could pass on this beautiful gift to the world, I had to heal an old wound: I had to forgive my father for he had raped me when I was a child, then later committed suicide in the most gruesome way.

I did forgive my father and I here declare:

> I have forgiven my father for raping me through a whole night and continuing despite my constant pleading for him to stop.
> I have forgiven him for later committing suicide by brutally slashing his throat, loins and chest.
> I have set myself free.

I sincerely wish, with all my heart, that the following 11 gifts of the spirit process will help you attract all the love you want and set you free of any limitations. If you will take them in, absorb them and embody them—and by that, I mean live them daily through your physical, mental and emotional bodies—I promise you will change your life for the better in miraculous ways.

Gift #1: Live Your Love

The more you can live the truth of your heart, the more you will be able to love yourself. Unconditional love is the way to inner peace and your soul's growth. With love, you will never be alone. Love attracts love, and you are *already* love, pure awareness, the field of unbounded love that everything appears in.

Exercise: Close your eyes and feel that unbounded love. Feel the shimmering energy field of your body, and know that that energy is love. Then channel that love into the present by writing down 1) everything you have done that you are proud of, and 2) everything you feel thankful for.

Gift #2: Live Your Courage

I have been in the darkest places in life and so filled with fear that I doubted whether I would ever find my way out. But after many years of searching, I found my path out of fear. Day by day, step by step, I have performed little acts of bravery that have helped to let courage, instead of fear, flow freely through my mind and body. I know that you can do the same.

Exercise: Describe your biggest fear. Imagine that you collect everything related to this fear and place it outside of yourself. Instead of identifying with your fear, take control of it and externalize it, setting yourself free of it. Do this for all the major fears you can identify. Also, begin a daily practice of doing something scary every day, starting with small things, like speaking up when you feel shy or asking for what you want. Notice the freedom and expansion that come.

Gift #3: Live Your Secrets

We all have had secrets at times. It is so important for your personal growth and your love for yourself that you dare to come clean about your secrets, at least to yourself and those involved, and own *all* of who you are, without excuses or masks. When you acknowledge yourself in all your aspects, light and dark, you live more truly in accordance with your essence, your inner light. When you tell your secrets, they simply lose their power over you, and you can live your truth.

Exercise: Describe who you are by inviting the true you into the light. Tell your real story.

Gift #4: Live Your Highest Vibration

The gratitude vibration is the highest vibration of all. When you live from within your highest vibration, your actions spring from the realm of light. The higher your vibration, the more in touch you become with your higher self and the more you are blessed with love, happiness and health.

Exercise: Every day write down at least five things you are grateful for.

Gift #5: Live Your Tribe

Your vibe attracts your tribe, your spiritual buddies, who help you to be in alignment with your true nature and feel unconditionally loved and accepted. The more you appreciate and love yourself, the more your tribe will love you and you will love them.

Exercise: Be specific about what you long for in community, and ask the universe to support your desire. Make eye contact with people and look past their surface appearances and deep into the beauty of their soul. Your tribe will show up and show you the way.

Gift #6: Live Your Inner Seer

Tap into the healing wisdom of your inner seer, from where your heart and soul speak to you in the quiet whisper between two thoughts. Intuition is the gift we don't always dare to open, as our doubt makes us fear it. Know that your intuition is a knowing you wake up with and should not deny. It's the doorway to creativity.

Exercise: Place a notepad by your bed. At bedtime, write down the questions you have. Next morning, soon after waking, tap into the healing wisdom of your intuition and you will get answers.

Gift #7: Live Your Inner Child

We all have within us a source of positive energy: our essence. Little children are brilliant at living in this energy and acting on their true, spontaneous feelings. They emanate the power of creation, which is naturally tuned in to the source energy and always turned toward the light. Give yourself the gift of finding the child within yourself and live your unique creativity. It will nourish your every cell.

Exercise: Scientists say, for true health, take 10 minutes a day to sing, laugh, dance and be playful. Tap into this bright energy every day.

Gift #8: Live Your Wealth

Wealth isn't measured only by money and possessions; it manifests in many forms in our lives. You can be wealthy in love, compassion, strength, energy, self-reliance and inner fulfillment. Your greatest wealth is your higher consciousness.

Exercise: Describe the wealth in your life that isn't based on money.

Gift #9: Live Your Magic

Magic is the power to manifest miracles through your intention. You have this power whenever you are in the flow of life, and you can use it to manifest your wishes in the world around you.

Exercise: Strengthen your powers of manifestation through practices that purify you and increase your ability to align with the flow of life. Create your own magic room with images of those who connect you with your manifesting power, whether they're angels, your elders and ancestors, your heroes and saints. Ask them for answers to the questions in your heart. The answers will come to you intuitively or in signs.

Gift #10: Live Your Silence

The greatest gift you can give yourself is just being still and listening to your soul. Know that your soul always knows what to do to heal itself. Your soul will tell you everything you ever need to know. Just listen.

Exercise: To connect with your inner silence, you need to control your breath. Breathing influences your autonomic nervous system and helps you connect with your soul. Breathe in slowly through your nose, feel your stomach expand, hold this breath for 10 seconds and then exhale slowly through your mouth. Repeat this 10 times, once a day.

Gift #11: Live Your Freedom

To liberate yourself, set yourself free of bad habits, dependencies and blockages. Then you can speak and live your true self. We can also free ourselves of victimhood, fears, anger, doubts and darkness by forgiving people who have wronged us. When we forgive, we shift our perception from anger and fear to love, and liberate our hearts and minds.

Exercise: Write down five things you want to free yourself of. What will you gain from this liberation? What will it allow you to become? Find at least one thing you are ready to forgive in each person you are close with.

It is with the greatest love and sense of honor,
that I pass on to you these 11 gifts,
which have helped so many to unblock their soul's purpose
and live a life of supreme love.

Today I am able to embrace my father's soul with boundless love. I have learned how important it is to liberate oneself from all fear and negativity. I now know that my father was my greatest teacher and that true love always leads us to the right path in life. Love is the only way.

 *Pia Nissen Tylak is a transformational leader, a Master Spirit Coach and a modern shaman sharing unconditional love. A former TV host, Pia ran her own creative business, employing more than 150 people, before following her passion. She is the visionary founder and spiritual director of The Spirit Academy, which trains Executive Spirit Coaches, who help people transform their lives. Through The Spirit Process she has helped thousands of people discover and fulfill their soul's purpose and live a life of supreme love.*

You can learn more about Pia and her programs for the unfolding of unconditional love at www.pianissentylak.com and www.pianissentylak.dk.

Chapter 18

Saying Good-bye Gracefully:
A New Perspective on Death
Susan Mercer

"The real question is not whether life exists after death.
The real question is whether you are alive before death."
—Osho

D on't let the title fool you. This chapter is really about life, as one cannot die without living, and one must be alive to die.

We are not eternal; we all come into this world with an expiration date. We just don't know what that date is. Today, tomorrow, next week, next month, next year…no one knows for sure when that day will come: it's the great mystery of life. And it's what we do with this mystery that creates our life. Do we live in fear and therefore never take risks? Do we live recklessly, thinking we're invincible? Do we live cautiously, afraid of getting hurt? Or do we live fully, embracing each and every day as if it's the last one in this dimension we call human life?

And then there's the question of the way we die. What if you could exit this dimension peacefully, without struggle, pain or fear? You may not be able to choose the way you die; however, you can change how afraid you are of it. It is the unknown of death that keeps us stuck in fear. Maybe the unknown doesn't need to be scary. As we create conversations around the topic of death and become more familiar with it, instead of ignoring it, we may then be able to shift our feelings about death.

We can choose to change our perspective about death. In the same way we all are capable of living well, we're also capable of dying well *if* we make a plan for how we want to die. You may not know the when or the how of your death; however, you can choose the way you spend your last days and breaths.

First, let's consider what it means to live well. I feel it means being present in the current moment and using all my senses, all the time, to embrace my surroundings. By doing this, I can live more fully. And by living fully, I am more accepting of my death because I've lived my life without regrets.

What does living well mean to you? It's an interesting question to ponder, isn't it?

One way to live fully is by experiencing all your senses continuously. You have the gift of sight to view the birds, trees, sky, insects, friends and lovers. The sense of smell can keep you lingering in enjoyment or blocking your nose. You may be taking in the aroma of a rose when a whiff of a garbage truck has you turning away. The scent of someone's perfume recalls the memory of a loved one who wore a similar fragrance.

Taste gives you the ability to make choices in what you eat and lets you enjoy sensations of sweet, sour and spicy. Do you savor each bite of food? Or do you eat just for nourishment, without paying attention to the flavor and texture and the feeling you get from the food?

Your sense of touch allows you to experience sensations, pleasant or painful, and protects you from harm. Touching a baby's arm or holding the hand of a loved one also gives you the feeling of connection. Feeling the wind gently caress you tells you what the air feels like.

And then, there's hearing, the last sense to leave the body. Even when you're unconscious, you can still hear, and a deaf person can tap into the vibration of life. Everything has energy and vibration. You can hear the music of life all around you, and it can add great richness to life.

Another essential component of living fully is this: we each need to live our life purpose and fulfill our heart's desire. Much like a flower and butterfly, you have a purpose for living right now at this time. The bud never questions its ability to become the flower, and the caterpillar never wonders if it should become the butterfly. They just know and come fully into their being. Do you live fully in your purpose of life, embracing the present moment with all five senses, or do you walk around unconsciously, perhaps living in the past or consumed with thoughts of the future?

So, what does all this have to do with death? Everything! Being present for your death is like being present in life. People fear death because they haven't experienced it or, if there are past lives, they don't remember the experience. It's an unknown, so many people are afraid of it. Yet, each day you're confronted by the unknown. Even if you have a routine you follow, something could disrupt that routine at any moment, and you would have to face the unknown. Imagine facing the unknown with curiosity instead of fear. Curiosity opens the doors that fear closes.

Just as it's possible to be curious and unafraid of life, you can also be curious and unafraid of death. Let's prepare for our last days in a way that brings more of the unknown into the light. One way is to create what I call a "Love/Death Plan." This is a plan outlining all your end-of-life wishes, for your loved ones and medical staff. It takes the guesswork out of the decision-making process at this emotional time.

For example, think about where you want to die: In a hospital, at a care facility or at home? What do you want your room to look like? If you are prepared and let your loved ones know your wishes, you can create your ideal place, and it doesn't have to look or feel institutional. You can have candlelight, flowers, music and incense. You can have your favorite poems and stories read to you. You can have aromatherapy, lotion, soft clothing, familiar pillows/blankets, photographs—anything you want to make your transition more comfortable and peaceful.

Also, after having discussions with your loved ones and doctors, think about what you want—and don't want—medically, and write your wishes down. Designate someone who will make sure your wishes are followed. Do you want to have a Do Not Resuscitate order (a DNR)? This question and many more are asked on Five Wishes, a great online resource listing important questions to consider as the end of your life draws near (https://agingwithdignity.org/five-wishes/about-five-wishes).

Good communication around the subject of death before the end can ease everyone's suffering and take some of the unknowns out of the equation. When there is less fear of death, these last days can really become more of an opportunity for everyone, including you, to celebrate your life.

Another way to prepare for your death is by creating a Legacy Project. Think about your contribution to the world, not just monetarily but by your presence in the world at this time. How do you want to be remembered by friends and loved ones? The Legacy Project is a "life in review" collection of tangible things you leave behind. These could include a scrapbook of favorite places traveled, letters to your loved ones, a book of favorite sayings or wisdom you want to share, videos capturing your life or maybe favorite recipes, just to name a few of the many things celebrating you and the life you have led.

This may also create an opportunity to connect with someone you haven't spoken to in a while, maybe to ask for forgiveness or to give it, to mend fences, to live without regrets. This would prevent the painful thoughts, *I wish I had...* or *I should have...* By thinking ahead to these legacy issues, perhaps you can die more peacefully.

As a part of the Legacy Project, you can also write your own obituary. What would you say? What would you want people to know about you? You could also plan your wake or funeral or memorial service. There are many options and decisions to make. Dry ice can maintain the body's appearance for three days, so there may be no need to be embalmed. You can rent a casket or ask family members and friends to decorate one. There are now "green" burial sites where only biodegradable containers are allowed. You can also incorporate your ashes with seeds to plant a tree or with coral to regenerate a coral reef. There are eco-friendly alternatives to many traditional practices.

Ancient civilizations celebrated the rite of passage from this dimension to the next with many elaborate ceremonies. Did they have it wrong? I think not. In the city of New Orleans, the lives of those now gone are celebrated with jazz music and a parade, which seems great to me. Yes, there is sadness that accompanies death, and there can also be joy that a life has been fully lived, enjoyed and completed.

"Regrets," as Frank Sinatra sang, "I've had a few, too few to mention…I did it my way!"

Isn't that what living well and dying well is really about? Living without regrets in a loving, caring and kind way, regardless of challenges, helps us die peacefully, without regrets.

What else holds us back from having a peaceful passing? Often, it's fear, anxiety, pain and the struggle to breathe. A wonderful antidote to all of these is the use of visualizations. Visualizations are helpful when dealing with fear and struggling for breath. This is effective because as someone is relating your visualization to you, your mind is focusing on the beauty of the place they are describing, and the cadence and sound of their voice takes you away from the pain and struggle into a place of calm, ease and serenity. The breath finds its previous rhythm and the body becomes less tense and relaxes. I also find them helpful when I'm feeling stressed. My favorite visualization looks like this:

The warm white sand beneath my feet and between my toes gives me the sense of being grounded in the earth. As I gaze at the turquoise waters, the warm rays of the sun embrace me in a gentle hug, filling me with serenity. The fragrant breeze rustling the fronds of the palm trees keeps me cool, calm and comfortable. I set down my orange blanket and pink chair in the perfect spot of seclusion under a low branch offering me soothing shade. I take a leisurely stroll down to the crystal clear, azure water and dabble my toes in the water. I can see the bottom of pure white sand and a few brave, colorful fish darting about.

Oh, how I love the warm yet refreshing water as it now laps against my ankles, beckoning me to come in deeper and deeper, until I find myself immersed in the tranquil sea. I stretch out, so buoyant I can gently float on the surface without much effort. The sounds of the water gently slapping against me fill me with wonderment and peacefulness. Floating on the ocean feels like floating on a cloud. Not a care in the world, no pain, no struggle—just beauty and ecstasy. Above and around me, pelicans soar. Dolphins are making their way to me easily, casually, swimming and sometimes jumping as they enjoy this most perfect day.

And I continue to float, easily, peacefully without a care in the world. Then I roll over on my stomach to observe the small zebra-striped fish in their glory of blues, yellows, reds and oranges, darting to and fro. Ah, now I venture back to the warmth of the sand and the sun and the gentle breezes caressing my body.

Can you feel the deep relaxation this brings? Hiking through the mountains may be another great adventure you can conjure up and enjoy at any time. You can write out your favorite visualization and have someone read it to you, or record it and listen whenever you want. Your breath slows, anxiety is released and pain subsides—for the reader as well as for the listener!

I encourage you to have some fun with this and be creative and explicit in your descriptions. As you become comfortable creating this visualization, imagine formulating your Love/Death Plan in much the same fun and creative way.

If you have religious beliefs, they will, of course, play an important role in how you perceive your death. My approach is based on my faith and spirituality. I feel I am living heaven on earth here and now and completing my mission of changing the way American society views death.

I feel anything and everything is possible in this life and in the hereafter, and it is up to each one of us to follow our own path and create the best life and death we can. I can feel we are not alone.

You may be thinking, *I'm healthy! Why would I want to think about this now?* While you're healthy is the perfect time, as you have the energy for it and can have fun and be creative with it. And in doing so, you'll ease the burden on your loved ones, who can't possibly know what you want if you haven't told them. This can be a worry and even a heartache for many. You are also setting an uplifting example and showing your loved ones that death need not be scary. This attitude opens up channels of discussion about how you and those dear to you perceive death, and this can create feelings of intimacy, trust and understanding, which are gifts in and of themselves. This is truly the celebration of your life, and it's a wonderful way to share in the celebration as you create your final chapter.

So now you have some tools to work with: the Love/Death Plan, which includes the Legacy Project, the visualization and your choice of where you want to be and what you want your space to feel like. Once you've created these pieces, the unknown has become more known. The mystery of death will always remain; however, the fear doesn't have to! I encourage you to create all of this while you're still able and healthy and can do it with humor, fun and creativity.

We organize our vacation plans, our travel plans and our will. This is a living plan to be created and shared while you're alive and then to be honored by family and friends when you depart from this dimension. It's a loving and joyful way to have a graceful good-bye.

Susan Mercer is an end-of-life doula, an intuitive/medium and an interior designer, and she has been a hospice volunteer. Susan takes the time to listen to each person's desires and assists them in making their decisions with clarity, thoughtfulness and love. Her experience in sitting vigil with clients through their end-of-life transition has led her to embrace the celebration of life while providing serenity during the transition. Her philosophy of having clients state their wishes in advance alleviates the fear of the unknown for her clients and their families. Her goal is to increase awareness of these concepts in the general public and also in the medical field. Susan can be reached at Susan@ modernoutlooks.com or at 508-221-8596.

Chapter 19

No Choice but Change:
Shifting from Fear to Love after Trauma
Helgi Maki

Some years ago, I accidentally discovered that my father was using the suits hanging in his bedroom closet as a secret liquor cabinet. Following the scent of alcohol in the air, I opened my father's closet and slipped my hand into the front pocket of one of his coat jackets. Nothing there. I tried the other side. My fingers hit glass; I pulled out a small bottle of vodka. My heart sank. I searched the other coats and found more bottles.

I had feared for many years that my father's drinking was more out of control than anyone had guessed. I had silently monitored the red flags: small bottles of alcohol rolling around under the driver's seat or in the glovebox of his car; canceled plans to visit me at the last minute because "he didn't want to inconvenience me"; his claims when we talked on the phone to be cooking grass-fed beef and organic greens from the local farmer's market for dinner, while he sounded like he was one breath away from the grave.

About a year later, on a muggy August day, I got the call from the police that my father had died from alcohol abuse. Instantly, I had the eerie feeling that I was about to be flooded with secrets I didn't want to know. Unfortunately, I was right. It seems he had been drinking himself to death ever since being released months before from the alcoholism rehabilitation facility he had been sent to after a drunk-driving charge.

I arrived at his house to find it filled knee-deep with empty 40-ounce vodka bottles. There was only a small path from room to room to navigate the mess, and mice had infested the chaotic piles of paper and clothing strewn around his home. The only food in his kitchen was a carton of spoiled milk. He had somehow hidden his condition and the state of his house from his family and friends for about two years.

Before that call from the police, each time a traumatic event had occurred with my father, I had scrambled to find a way to ignore or hide the effects the trauma had had on me. But I couldn't do that this time. I had to go to the police station to pick up a plastic bag of his personal effects because his house was being investigated as a possible crime scene. I had to deal with the cold truth and could no longer pretend to be able to handle the trauma or fake that I knew what to do. I became frequently overcome with the fear that I wouldn't be able to find a way to cope effectively with this loss.

Even worse, I had to give the news of his death to my mother. For years, she had appeared to be fairly functional, but I knew she was secretly suffering from her own traumatic experiences, which had left her with severe clinical depression. Having to tell my mother this tragic news felt like an impossibly cruel task—and one I feared I was completely unqualified to handle.

As I flew across the country to tell her in person, I thought endlessly about how to deliver the news without increasing her suffering. I also wondered if anything good could ever happen in my life again—or whether all my worst fears would come true as this one had. I felt my heart and all my insides sink, as I thought about the pain we'd both feel when I would have to say, "He drank himself to death." Maybe I could put it less harshly, but that was how other people had described the situation, and it seemed to me to be sadly accurate.

Challenged to Change

> *"When we are no longer able to change a situation,*
> *we are challenged to change ourselves."*
> **—Viktor E. Frankl**

When I arrived at my mother's door, I still had no idea how to tell her the awful news without making us both suffer more. As she opened the door and I looked into her eyes, I could feel how angry we both were at the unfairness of his addiction. We were two tidal waves of fear and anger about to collide. Seeing her pain, I felt a desperate and selfish need to reduce my own suffering.

But, as I opened my mouth to speak, something altogether new and different started to awaken from deep within me. It was a feeling I had never known before. Foreign-sounding words came from my mouth in the softest and most loving voice. I reached out, softly held her shoulder to steady her and said, "I'm so sad to tell you this, Mom. Please sit down with me."

Who was this new inner person who was so loving and compassionate?

I didn't know her, but I had an idea of where she had come from. Shortly before my father's death, I had read Viktor Frankl's book *Man's Search for Meaning*. It's a famously life-changing book in which Frankl bravely recounts his experience as a concentration camp prisoner during the Holocaust and makes deeply insightful observations about how he and others were able to live under, and after, those most dire of circumstances. The trauma he experienced in the Holocaust was a whole other universe of trauma, far beyond what I had ever encountered, but somehow he had grown profoundly from it.

Now, speaking to my mother, I was discovering that I had been irrevocably changed by Frankl's words about a person's ability to choose their attitude, regardless of circumstance. He wrote, "Everything can be taken from a man but one thing: the last of the human freedoms—to choose one's attitude in any given set of circumstances, to choose one's own way."

As I continued to speak to Mom, I found myself in new territory. I talked to her about Dad's life more kindly than I had ever thought to before, as one riddled with dysfunction because of his own father having been physically violent. I pointed out that he had loved us and that, given his troubled early life, what could we expect but that he might turn to addiction as a way to numb his pain? I said he had seemed to try very hard to stop drinking, but, despite his best efforts, the disease of alcoholism had taken over.

I looked into my mother's eyes after my explanation and saw that they were less charged with anger but still dark with pain. And then, unexpectedly, my mouth opened and out popped words I had never said before, especially in relation to my family or misfortune of any type: "The only way through this is with love and understanding." In that moment, I unexpectedly verbalized the attitude I would continue to choose to take toward this unchangeable circumstance. I would try to love and understand my way through it, as challenging and foreign as that sounded to me at the time.

When I finished talking, my mother was silent. I was silent, too. I had said things that sounded crazy to me, things I hadn't felt even a millisecond before I began to speak. Just moments before, I had been feeling all the usual feelings of grief: I was in denial, I was bargaining with God to try to magically get my dad's life back, I was terrified, I was full of sad and disturbing memories and I was mad as hell at life. Now, I was in an entirely different place.

And then, to my surprise, my mother quietly agreed with me. We would get through this with love and understanding—even though we had not one idea how to do that, other than stating our intention to do so.

Facing the Challenge to Change after Trauma

Well, it's one thing to pick an attitude toward trauma or loss in a moment and another to live that attitude on a daily basis. Even though I needed and wanted to make my sudden change in attitude permanent, I had great difficulty doing it consistently. In the coming days and weeks my mind roiled with negative, fearful thoughts. *Why couldn't I have seen how extreme his drinking was and stopped it? Why had he become so impossible to deal with—lying and driving drunk and even threatening me with physical violence? Was my life going to end in suffering, too?*

I appeared to be successful in my career as a lawyer and in life. But inside I was overwhelmed by grief, fear, despair and shame. And these feelings only grew when, a few years after my father's death, my mother died from an overdose of prescription drugs. The loss of her shook me to the core at every level of my being. Another of my worst fears had been realized, and again I felt like I might be condemned to a life of fear and tragedy.

But I quickly realized I couldn't let that happen. I decided I would try to edge closer to the attitude I called "love and understanding" by asking myself every day whether there was something that I could love or understand even one tiny little bit more than I had before. I didn't try to avoid or diminish my natural feelings, but I did plant seeds of change as I gathered these bits of love and understanding as they came to my mind. For instance, I could love thinking of my dad's ridiculously funny jokes or remembering his lively acoustic guitar music. I could love that he gave the best bear hug around, even when we weren't getting along. I could understand that I had tried my best to show both my mother and father that I loved them every chance I got.

I kept collecting these small points of love and understanding daily, and I found that they made me feel noticeably better. I felt a fragment of peace and a lessening of fear every time I found something I was willing to understand or love, even for a brief moment. And these bits of peace and love and understanding started to create a sort of balance in my life.

Practicing the Change You Have Chosen

As I searched for other ways to heal, I found that my practice of gathering bits of love was similar to a Buddhist mindfulness practice described by Thich Nhất Hạnh as "inviting positive seeds." He describes this practice in his book *No Mud, No Lotus,* as follows: "One way of taking care of our suffering is to invite a seed of the opposite nature to come up. As nothing exists without its opposite, if you have a seed of arrogance, you also have a seed of compassion… We can selectively water the good seeds and refrain from watering the negative seeds."

I found that the best way to create the conditions for something other than fear and pain to exist in my life was to feel non-fear and non-pain (which for me was understanding and love) in my mind and body. Each time I proved to myself that love exists—just by feeling it for a few moments—I reduced the amount of time I felt fear and pain. At first I could only be without fear and pain for half an hour at a time, but after a while I was able to hold understanding and love within myself for longer stretches of time.

Here's a meditation I created that you can try on your own to grow the seeds of love in your mind and heart, and reduce your fear and pain. I suggest recording it on your phone, listening to it every day and following the instructions.

The Loving-Moments Meditation

This is a meditation to reduce fear and pain by increasing love.

I find a quiet place where I am comfortable.

Before I begin the meditation, I think of three loving moments in life when I experienced a very simple sensation that I love. It's best to pick a very simple sensation or thing that can be experienced with the sense of sight, hearing, touch, taste or smell, such as seeing a favorite color, tasting a delicious spice, touching a friendly animal, hearing enjoyable sounds or smelling clean air.

Once I have selected my three loving moments, I begin the meditation by relaxing and scanning my body for any sensations I can feel for a slow count of 30. I am free from judgment as I notice those sensations, simply sensing how my body feels today. (Count slowly to 30.)

And now I recall my first loving moment, remembering the sensation of sight, sound, taste, smell or touch that I loved. For a slow count of 10, I experience that moment for myself in this meditation, as if it is happening right now. (Count slowly to 10.)

And now I pause to notice how that loving moment feels in my body. I notice whether there are any sensations in my body from the loving moment, and how they feel. And finally after I hold and notice those sensations for a moment I release them and simply become aware of how I feel in my body after experiencing that moment of love.

I repeat this loving moment-meditation two more times, reading the above two paragraphs again for the other two simple sensations of love I have chosen.

After I have done the loving-moment meditation for each of my three simple pleasures, I pause one last time, noticing how I feel now, compared to the beginning of the meditation.

And then I imagine that the sun has just come out and sunlight is shining on my skin. The sun is giving me a sense of warmth as it shines. I feel sunlight shining around me for a slow count of 15. (Count to 15.)

Finally, I begin to gently move my body and thank myself for appreciating the existence of the sensation of love.

Thanks to this meditation and the regular practice of growing positive emotional seeds, I'm no longer preoccupied by negative, fear-driven thoughts. Instead of seeing trauma as a ruinous situation, I see it as a call to respond authentically to an unchangeable situation, including reevaluating my core beliefs and embarking on personal changes as necessary. In this way, the losses I had to endure have inspired me to live more fully each day.

Today, I enjoy a happier life than I ever could have imagined. In fact, to my surprise, I'm happier than I was before I encountered trauma. I'm deeply grateful that the cycle of trauma has been broken, and I know that my parents would be, too. To my amazement and delight, in my life, on most days, love has won.

Helgi Maki believes it is possible to find a unique path to personal happiness, even after complete and utter disaster in life. She is a lawyer, writer and teacher of mindfulness and movement practices to cultivate happiness and vitality after trauma. She specializes in helping people who have encountered traumatic events effectively make the transition to living fully and meaningfully again, using multiple tools to shift toward post-traumatic growth, integration, self-compassion, long-term acceptance, resilience and a sense of discovery. She writes because she feels compelled to give words to the specifics of the unspoken transition often demanded of people affected by trauma, including mental illness and addiction, and to reduce stigma. Helgi can be found at www.happyafterdisaster.com.

Chapter 20

A Trail of Tears Leads to a Road of Recovery
Michele Bray MacNair

The night had started out like a beautiful dream. It was like the night Cinderella went to the ball at the palace, with hundreds of finely dressed guests, maids with starched black-and-white outfits, butlers and serving men, a lovely orchestra, fabulous hors d'oeuvres, the beautiful bride and groom, grand staircases, oriental carpets, clinking glasses and me, in awe of the fancy event.

My Cinderella Mother was all the rave at the palace-mansion, in a swirling white cotton summer dress of eyelet lace, with a fabulous wide-brimmed white hat and slippers almost like glass. I had always been seduced by Mom's voice, her dashing black eyes, her wavy black hair, her full crimson lips and her engaging smile that showed off her perfect white teeth. To this heart and mind, Mom was a beautiful Choctaw princess, and I was in love with her every move, swing and twinkle. She danced divinely!

Then, on the way home, the beautiful dream turned into a nightmare.

Like the fairy tale of old, we three little mice, ages eight, five and three, turned into three young children—my sister, my brother and me, all afraid and confused by the vomiting and groaning of their Cinderella Mother. The orange pumpkin dissolved into our dark green Hudson sedan, which rolled to a stop along a darkened boulevard in suburban Beverly Hills, where Mom tossed her cookies into the gutter. She was drunk, without any dignity and without being conscious of the humiliation she was heaping upon us and, more to the point, upon me, her eldest child. I was the one who saw her moaning and slumped over with spittle foaming from her lips.

It was me, crying and choking on words filled with anger and hate, who was vehement with disgust and in a rage that I couldn't disguise. Dad tried to help Mom as she sprawled out over the floorboards of the car, puking and puking onto the street. I was ashamed—so ashamed—and mortified. The awful moaning mixed with the sound of vomit, kept me awake for endless nights of hate and disgust and feeling so disillusioned about my mom.

Once home, Dad carried Mom into the bathroom, where she continued to vomit and pee on herself, on the floor and on her lovely white dress. Mom was no longer *my* Cinderella princess. Not now. Maybe never.

This hideous incident consumed me as I grew into an adult, but it certainly wasn't the only time Mom was drunk when I was a child. She came home from work and drank, and she was drunk most of every weekend. Walking home from school, I was always in a panic over what I'd find at home.

Coming home from school at age 12, I tried to anticipate how the rest of the day might be. It was like a TV show we often watched, *Peter Potter's Platter Parade*, where you guessed if a song he played was a "hit" or a "miss." I tried to guess if our house was a hit or a miss. Was Mom in the house somewhere, drunk or passed out in a darkened room, or was she sober, with the drapes open and the sun shining in everywhere? I was always in a frenzied state of agitation.

Whenever Dad took Mom out, he enabled her (that is, unintentionally aided her alcoholism), and she always got plastered. He had to half-carry her into the house, as she was unable to walk. I knew she would come in drunk. I waited up for them, so angry, and the minute they arrived, I dashed into the hall and pounced like a wildcat, screaming, "I hate you, I hate you." Dad always tried to quiet me and tell me to go to bed, but I was too riled up. I hated my Dad for letting her get so intoxicated. I despised her for having no control.

In my insanity, I searched all over the house for hidden brandy bottles. I found them in her drawers, and inside her shoes, in the pocket of a coat. I even found one in a Kotex box and one in the water tank of the toilet. I felt it my duty to look and find them and then pour all the booze down the drain.

I never had friends come over or sleepovers at our house. I never had dates come and pick me up at home. Mother, who had been my idol as a little child, was continuing to make our home life a hell with her alcoholism. I was always in fear of Mom's inebriation and slurred words—making no sense with her sentences. I was stressed out and always apprehensive.

When Mom was drunk, which was also most evenings after she came home from her work as a hairdresser, it was as though a cruel alien had scooped me up and tossed me into the world of a fearful movie I'd seen on TV called *The Snake Pit*, starring Olivia de Havilland. It was about a young woman who was thrown into an insane asylum with other dark and frightening women. I had a terrible fear that Mom would somehow end up in one of those wretched hospitals, all alone.

Too young to know how to handle all of my intense emotions toward my mom, I became a total hypochondriac. From the age of 12, I thought I had every disease I knew existed. If my heart beat too fast, I was having a heart attack; when I couldn't breathe, I figured I was close to convulsions. When my legs ached after swimming, I had polio. This lasted through my 20s, but, whenever I went to a doctor, he found no debilitation or disease. It took years to discover I was having panic attacks—a condition I'd never heard of before. At the time, the doctors probably thought I was nuts.

My dad and my brother probably also saw me as Looney Tunes. Dad, however, always consoled me, held me and let me share my fears of my impending death with him. Thoughts of my own life-threatening illnesses were how I tried to banish thoughts of the reception night.

It hadn't always been this way. The mother I knew as a little girl, before alcoholism took her over, was a joyous woman who loved her kids and loved to sing. From my earliest years, she sang—lullabies, big band tunes, folk songs, religious songs, ditties. Mom had a lovely alto voice and a remarkable memory for words to songs. We all listened to the *Platter Parade* on TV and memorized all the popular songs of the '50s. We kids sang them for hours on our backyard swing, and we sang them as a family.

Singing with my mother was like a religion to me. When she wasn't drinking, just the two of us would often be in the sunny kitchen with my mom ironing away, the two of us just waiting for the next song to thrill our hearts. For me, it was always magical to have my mother all to myself, even if I shared her with the damp laundry. It was her vivid imagination I loved, ready to leap into a new song or a lost one from her past.

But harder times came with adolescence. When I was in high school, I told my best friend that my private theme song was "Only the Lonely" by Roy Orbison, and it made her cry. Like many kids that age, I felt completely alone, depressed and terribly confused by how nonexistent I felt. Hungry for love and acknowledgement and afraid of other people's criticism, I could barely talk with most of the kids at school. When I had a boyfriend, I was so needy, I usually only thought about myself and rarely about "us."

Later in life, I learned Mom had lived a childhood filled with her own kind of dread and trepidation. Mom's mom, Martha, a Choctaw Indian, and her dad, Acy, were divorced. He had visitation rights with the two children. When Mom was six years old, her dad came to the house and collected her and her little brother Johnny for their usual visit with him, or so they thought. Instead, he stole the two kids, taking them far away to Arizona.

Acy never contacted Martha, and she had no idea where her children had disappeared to or what had become of them. A few days after he stole the kids away, he told Mom that her mother had died, so she and Johnny were coming to live with him. What a shock that was for her! Confusion reigned in her heart and mind. Her mother was everything to her.

Sometimes when Mom was sober, she told me her favorite memories. Some were of her mother taking her on a path into the local woods to scout for herbs and medicinal plants. Mom told me how she had loved the quiet days when she and her mother hunted for herbs and lay for hours in the grass, looking at animals and talking and cuddling together in deep solitude and harmony. Martha had the gift to be quiet and loving in the Choctaw way that Mom had, too, when she wasn't drunk.

Mom's life with Acy was hard. He sometimes drank heavily and then was abusive to Mom and Johnny. When he was broke, more than once he dropped the children off at an orphanage, where they received meals and a bed to sleep in. Mom never knew when he was going to pick them up, and a few times, they stayed there for three to four weeks. During those bleak periods, Mom missed her mother terribly. She pined for Martha and her Indian ways.

At age 17, Mom met our dad and married him after knowing him for only three weeks. When she was 18, she got word that Acy had died, and, around the same time, she heard from an aunt the shocking news that her mother was not dead but alive in Oklahoma City!

Mom told us this news hit her like a bolt of lightning and left her both glad that her mother was alive and furious with her. Why hadn't Martha looked for her and Johnny? She discovered later that Martha *had* looked for them, spending a lot of time and money having detectives search for them for over 10 years. But Acy had changed his name and address frequently, and the detectives hadn't been able to locate them.

Mom wondered her whole life how her own father could have told two small children that their mother was dead, and then dragged them across the country to live in strange and often pitiful places. She was too ashamed to tell me that Acy had molested her when she was a child; she said "a stranger" had done that, in a candy store.

But, even in the worst of times, one great thing that defined Mom was her hope for a better life. She spent years trying to get sober, going from one halfway house to another—and from one drunken night to another morning of regrets.

I am grateful to be able to say that, after many years of searching, Mom did find her way to a sober life and a spiritual path that eased her troubled heart. She discovered a church to belong to, friends to share her life with and a God to believe in, who also believed in her.

Today, I'm grateful to Mom, and because of that, I know you too can transform your experience if you've felt devastated by a loved one. Though I had barely graduated from high school due to the stresses at home, I was trained in special education and with that knowledge I began to see my mother as a whole person, not just the alcoholic terror I had often hated—or the beautiful songbird

I had always loved. She was a wonderful woman who ultimately found her way through the emotional wreckage of the multiple abandonments she had suffered in her early years—plus the curse of alcoholism and sexual abuse—to finally come home to a place of hope and love and endurance.

In teaching, I learned that a person with a disability is not defined wholly by that disability. He or she is not "an autistic child" but "a child with autism." I found that you're able to see the truth of a person, like Mom, when you're able to see the whole human being, the unique and worthy person who has the disability or disease.

I am who I am because I had perseverance and hope to look to, and I was blessed not to have inherited Mom's alcoholism. My soul was able to heal, and I became a person of positive convictions and resiliency. I now have belief when there is an abyss before me. Like Mom, I am tenacious. I work hard and, having created who I am through small steps on my own path, I am fully aware of my blessings.

I was able to learn these lessons early in my adult life, such that I could become an artist and a special education teacher, and enjoy having art shows and the respect of my peers and a good life, teaching students with disabilities. I had hope for our future, and my song was now "Good Day Sunshine" by the Beatles. I played that song every morning for years, and I felt the truth of it.

All of this was possible because I let go of Mom's past failings. If you are having trouble accepting and letting go of a loved one's past, I ask you to try to see the whole person. When you can see the big picture of your own life and of their life, too, your vision clears, your path becomes discernable and you can see that, truly, "Love is a Many-Splendored Thing."

Like many Choctaws of the past and present, I have retained my character and identity through times difficult to manage. I have been a practicing member of Al-Anon for 25 years, and I try to live "One Day at a Time." I honor my mom, who tried so hard for so many years and finally did succeed at becoming sober and content. I celebrate her for traits many Choctaws embrace. In her last 10 years, she was sensitive, compassionate and deeply loving to others.

My prayer is that you, too, will be able to see the larger picture of any person who's caused you grief, so that your life can be richer and fuller from that broader perspective. Know that one cannot walk in the moccasins of another, but, nonetheless, we can appreciate their walk and, for a time, walk beside them.

Michele Bray MacNair is a retired special education teacher. She spent 30 years teaching students with multiple disabilities and was the inclusion consultant for Santa Clara County Office of Education. Michele received an award as Teacher of the Year from a highly respected organization, Parents Helping Parents. She helped bridge the gap in inclusion for students with severe disabilities. Special education students were finally included in mainstream classes with typical students.

After taking a part-time job in a class for disabled students, Michele began to study education. She displayed talent, curiosity and a lust to give an education to children long forgotten, as they remained in the background of education and society. Michele also earned BA, MA and MFA degrees in art. She painted and did ceramics, and had art shows across the U.S. and in other countries. Michele currently mentors special education teachers earning their credentials.

Chapter 21

Stop Hiding and Start Living: How to Turn Adversity into an Asset

Dr. Ron Holt

I've always been afraid to share my story publicly, but I never want any youth to go through what I went through. Even now, after all these years, there are still young people who choose suicide because they aren't being accepted for who they are. I cannot remain silent any longer.

I'm a gay man, happily married to the man I love, making a good living as a psychiatrist and feeling very fortunate to be living in a progressive city like San Francisco. This is a place where I feel comfortable to be open and enjoy career, financial and relationship success. But let me assure you, it wasn't always this way.

My earliest memories of being different from the other boys go all the way back to the sixth grade. It was then I knew I was different, but I didn't know how to put a label on it. In my teenage years, I realized I was gay but struggled tremendously with this newfound reality and never officially came out as a gay person to anyone. But my secrecy didn't stop my father from tormenting me. He would frequently bully me and call me names like "fag" as I was growing up.

After years of this abuse, I was depressed, anxious and isolated. When I told my dad that I had thoughts of killing myself because of his words, he would say, "Go ahead. You don't have the balls to do it." I adopted the beliefs that the world was inherently bad, no one could be trusted and the only way to survive was to hide who I truly was—even from myself.

In college, I began to feel a slight bit of room to acknowledge my deepest feelings, but I still felt it was essential for my survival to hide my sexuality from others. During this time, I did begin dating a man but only in complete secrecy. After graduating, I went on to medical school and still worried that someone might discover my deep secret. I had mistakenly come to equate being gay with being weak and had no intention of coming out to anyone.

But things rarely go as we plan. It was a cold December day when I called my father to arrange my usual trip back to Nebraska for the holidays. My father lapsed into one of his all too familiar gay-bashing tirades, talking about someone else in a hateful way. He had done this many times before, but, on this day, something woke up inside of me. Rather than listen passively as usual, I told him that I didn't agree with the way he was stereotyping others. This simple comment led to more conversation, and, before I knew it, my dad asked me point-blank if I was gay.

I had rehearsed this moment endless times over the years, but in spite of all my planning I was completely thrown off guard. Never in a million years had I thought of coming out to my father over the phone. But a deep voice inside of me rose up and, with all the courage I could muster, I blurted out, "Yes!"

Then I thought, *What did I just do?*

"Fine!" my dad responded. "You have chosen this life, and you are never welcome home again!" And he hung up the phone.

A powerful wave of deep calm and inner peace came over me. It was like nothing I had ever experienced before. Finally, I was able to be true to myself and to my father. I thought to myself, *If losing my family allows me to be open and honest about who I am, then it's worth the price.* Even though I wasn't going home for Christmas that year, I was rejoicing deep in my soul. I was reborn that day and could finally start to live as my true, authentic self.

Transformative as this experience was, it was also the start of one of the most challenging periods of my life. Soon after I came out to my father, he started making harassing phone calls, each time leaving intense and at times threatening voicemails. They ranged from him wanting me to hear my mom hysterically wailing in the background to him informing me that he was contacting an attorney to change my last name, because of the shame and embarrassment I had brought to the family.

I still felt empowered by having come out to him, but his words nonetheless fortified the deep belief I still had that this was what society at large felt about gay people. His next phone call was a message that the rest of the family was going to be tested for HIV, as being gay somehow equated to having the virus. As the days progressed, the voicemails escalated to become even more frightening. He threatened to out me to my entire medical school administration in the hope that I would be expelled from school.

And then my father descended to a place I would never have thought possible between a father and his son: he threatened to kill me. And my partner. That message sent chills down my spine. Since my partner was living in the same city as my family at that time, I immediately called to warn him. He was in medical school but skipped classes, packed a bag and drove to Missouri to be with me. Unfortunately, we let our fear get the best of us. We then fled my apartment because we were afraid my father might drive to Missouri to kill us.

We went into hiding at a nearby hotel. With little money and no plan for what to do next, we frantically searched for help to deal with this craziness. We finally found a gay-affirmative pastor, who sat down to talk with us. After our conversation, he said he would reach out to my father on our behalf. He did speak with him, but my father was bent on destroying our lives. The pastor later told us he had never spoken to someone so full of anger.

The harassing phone messages continued multiple times a day. Finally, after a few more days, we were feeling as though we couldn't run any longer, so we returned to my apartment. We felt alone and afraid. We sat on my sofa together and talked about joint suicide. It was in this place of fear and despair that a tiny flame of light and strength was ignited within me. We decided not to end our lives that night.

The next time my father called, I harnessed this newfound strength and interrupted his tirade. I told him that if he threatened us again, I'd go to the police to report his behavior and obtain a restraining order against him. Finally, I stood up to him. And, as is often the case with bullies when their violence is exposed and others stand up to them, he crumbled into a heap of his own fear and shame. My father never harassed us again after that day.

Several years later, while we were still out of touch, my father suddenly died. I was left with a sense of sadness that he had never been able to love me for who I am.

Even though I was out to my family at this time, I was still closeted to most of the world. I began working as a clinical psychiatrist shortly after finishing my residency training in San Francisco. Working for a large medical corporation initially gave me a sense of anonymity that allowed me to keep my sexual orientation private. But as the years progressed, I began to see there was more work for me to do in self-acceptance and self-love. All of the training I'd received to help other people heal wasn't going to do me any good until I was first able to heal myself.

Often society expects that, somehow, a psychiatrist is going to have it all together. But I learned that I had to go through my own personal healing in a way that no structured training could ever teach. I had to transcend the very field I was trained in. I have a doctorate in healing, but I'm here to tell you that the most important thing I've come to learn about healing has nothing to do with biochemistry or pharmaceuticals, or Freud, Jung or anyone else. The most important thing I've learned is this: you cannot heal if you are hiding.

After I stopped hiding and began working through those horrendous experiences with my father, I was able to begin to embrace who I was at a deeper level. In the following years of extensive personal work, I began a transformation toward self-acceptance and self-love. Although this work is far from complete, I've profoundly improved my sense of self-worth and come to believe that the most challenging adversities in life can be transformed into the most powerful assets. I can say with confidence that this type of transformation can be an amazingly empowering journey.

Let me share some tips with you on how to transform the adversities in your life into assets.

Tip #1: You Cannot Heal If You Are Hiding

After coming out to my father, I felt like a new man. Although his reaction was one I would never wish upon anyone, I wouldn't change the opportunity to come out from hiding. Looking back on that time, I can see that hiding who I was had been making me feel even worse and more prone to pain and stress.

As humans, we all have truths that we are afraid to come out with, and we've all been worried about disappointing others. And that's true whatever you're hiding. It might be your sexual orientation or gender identity, your love for someone else, abuse you may have endured, the need to end a relationship because you can't be your authentic self or many other things. But, despite these fears, you must speak up. Because you cannot heal and become your true, authentic self until you stop hiding.

And the good news is that the courage to be authentic is something we all have, even when it feels, at best, like a faint flicker of light buried deep within. That courage is there because, at our core, we know that true healing—and our true lives—can never begin until we are free to be open about who we are.

Tip #2: Forgiveness Is a Gateway to Peace of Mind

Although I will never forget, I have come to forgive my father for not giving me unconditional love. Maybe he had never been given unconditional love himself. I realize now that, for whatever reason, my father simply didn't have the capacity to be the person I needed or wanted him to be. For many years, I held on to a deep resentment and even hatred toward him. But I've slowly come to the realization that my resentment and hatred weren't hurting him: they were only hurting me. I found I couldn't move forward with my life until I forgave him. So, I feel grateful that, today, I can say, "Father, I have forgiven you."

We all know what it's like when we hold on to feelings of anger, resentment or hurt. These feelings might eat away at us for days, years or even an entire lifetime if allowed, and we just end up suffering when we can't release them. In order to heal we must realize that, even though we can't change the way someone has treated us, we *can* change the way we respond to their behavior. When we release resentment and anger, we are then able to take back the power we had surrendered. *One of life's great paradoxes is that we can regain our personal power only when we can forgive the other person.*

You don't have to forget what happened, but moving forward with forgiveness brings deep healing. Forgiving someone is not for their benefit but for your own. Letting go of negative feelings gives you the profound freedom to move forward and fill that once-negative space with feelings of love, and it's a boundless type of love that transcends the individual self. Forgiveness opens up the space for renewed relationships with yourself, with others and perhaps even with the person who hurt you.

Sometimes the tables are turned and we may have hurt someone else. In these situations, forgiveness is an important part of the healing that we can offer to those we have injured. First, we need to forgive ourselves; only then are we able to lead the other person into a process of their healing. We do this when we ask the other person to forgive us. This is not mainly for our benefit; rather it's an invitation for the other person to experience the powerful and transformative healing that occurs when forgiving someone.

Tip #3: Empowerment Comes from Sharing Our Truth

After coming out and eventually forgiving my father, I decided to turn the lessons I'd learned into an asset to help others. Although gay rights and awareness have come a long way from the time when I came out, there are still millions of people who struggle with their sexual orientation or gender identity. So, for the past several years, I have been traveling back to colleges in the Midwest to give presentations on lesbian, gay, bisexual and transgender issues.

I have to admit I was initially terrified to speak on the subject I'd been so frightened of back when I was a student. However, over the years of giving these presentations, I've come to embrace the adversities I had as a young, gay, closeted male. I've worked to turn those painful experiences into an asset by helping others understand that they are not alone and their sexuality is just as natural as anyone else's. I have experienced tremendous growth, empowerment and self-love over the years by sharing what was once hidden in plain sight: my true, authentic self.

We each have unique knowledge, skills and abilities that can be used to help others, but sometimes it's the adversities in our lives that turn out to be our biggest assets. Sharing an adversity and letting others see what you've experienced can be frightening, but, with time, it will be empowering for both you and the recipient of your message. You can share your message in countless ways. The important thing is to speak out about your adversity and be open to the ways it can help you and others learn and grow.

I've come so far from my days of living in fear and hiding who I am. I hope my story helps you stop guarding any secrets you might have—and start living a truly authentic and fulfilling life.

 *Dr. Ron Holt is a licensed, board-certified psychiatrist and a motivational speaker, author and facilitator who resides in San Francisco, California. He is the #1 bestselling author of* PRIDE: You Can't Heal If You're Hiding from Yourself. *Ron is passionate about issues relevant to the Lesbian, Gay, Bisexual and Transgender (LGBT) communities and is a leader in the LGBT happiness and mental health world.*

Ron travels the country providing transformational education and mentoring to help people lead more authentic lives. He inspires people with breakthrough methods to help them achieve greater personal fulfillment. His style is approachable and relatable, and he is dedicated to helping people live more empowered and joy-filled lives.

Ron is the author of other books for LGBT youth and adults and their allies. You can learn more about Ron's books, videos and presentations at DrRonHolt.com or AudacityOfPride.com. Please feel free to contact Ron for additional information or to discuss ways he can assist your organization or school.

— *Chapter 22* —

Touching the Soul:
Entering the Realm of Connected Resonance
John Tolmie

H ave you ever felt connected with somebody who meant a lot to you? Maybe it even felt like your inner vibration matched theirs, and you could resonate with them at a deep level? If you have, I'll bet it was one of the great times of your life. And, I wonder, did feeling that deep connection make you believe that you'd never feel alone or unworthy of being loved again?

Was it pretty disappointing when that didn't happen?

I know it was for me. For many years, I searched for meaningful relationships, and when I found them, I looked to them for a sense of recognition and approval, and just to make myself feel more worthy. It took me years to realize that I had to get that feeling of worthiness from inside myself.

During those years, I was working professionally as a social worker, and I loved it. What I didn't see coming was that all the giving I was doing would slowly drain me of having a feeling of fulfillment of my own inner needs. When it came to decisions of whether to help others or myself, I chose others. Plus, I got addicted to positive feedback, and when I didn't get the feedback I felt I deserved, I crashed. Sometimes I overreacted and felt deceived and misled by people. I felt like I was a victim and didn't take any kind of responsibility for my feelings, and so my life had to go the way it did: downhill.

By 1997, my self-esteem was totally gone. I felt so sorry for myself that my girlfriend left me. I went into a deep depression. I felt alone and unhappy and had a strong sense of fear. I felt I was nothing, the same way I felt as a child when my father beat me and locked me up in a room, so I wouldn't be around and observing his drinking habits. But it turned out that there was a big upside to being alone, fearful and unhappy: I finally came to see that something was basically wrong with this picture!

I saw it like this. Imagine, if you will, the most important people in your life all lined up in a row. Take some time to picture this. Can you see them? Who is in the picture? Now let me ask you the question, are *you* in the picture? If not, do you see how off-kilter this is? You have left yourself off the list of the most important people in your life. Do you agree that you've got some work to do to get yourself back into the picture, into balance, and to see yourself in a better way?

Have you got it? Okay, now, picture yourself standing beside them, in that row. Ask yourself, do you have the same positive feelings for yourself that you have for the others? If not, what's missing? What would it be like if you saw yourself as being as important as the most important people in your life?

For me, this small exercise revealed how unworthy I felt; it was actually hard for me to imagine myself in that row of people at all! Something was truly missing in the relationship I had with myself. I saw that, up until the depression hit me, I hadn't counted myself in. Not at all. You know how the flight attendant on an airplane asks you to put on your own mask before you help children and others? I had been doing the opposite my whole life. So, of course, I always ran out of air and lost myself along the way.

Does that maybe sound familiar?

When I realized this had to change, everything began to change. I had to learn to care about myself the way I cared for others. Today I am humbly thankful for my depression because it made me stop and consider my responsibility to "grow myself." Since then I have worked every day to gain greater insight into how I, and humans in general, perceive the world around us and, most of all, within us. I've studied how we can communicate more efficiently and connect on a deeper level with others and with ourselves.

That's been great, but when you're working on yourself, there can still be times of feeling insecure, and that was me in the middle of October 2013. I was locked up in an internal struggle and decided to have a session with my good friend and life mentor, the Vedic astrologer Terry Ray Johnson. When we talked, Terry told me that I would experience certain turmoil for around three to four weeks and then, he said, an angel would come to my rescue and offer me insights beyond anything I have ever experienced. The angel would take me through the storm to an everlasting peace within.

To be quite honest, this description was so far out that I thought it was never going to happen. As the weeks went by and my internal struggle wasn't getting any better, I called Terry again and asked for another conversation. On the morning of November 28, 2013, I was about to have the call with Terry when I noticed that it was a very magical morning outside and the sun was about to rise. I looked out the window to get a glimpse of the first rays of the sun approaching the horizon. The very moment the sunbeams touched the horizon and sparkled into my eyes, Terry's call came through. It was a moment of deep, meaningful synchronicity. Terry told me that a breakthrough was very near, and even though I still felt torn down inside, I believed that something beautiful and good was about to happen. When the call was over, I felt like things were beginning to fall into place, but I still had a sense of fear, too.

Then, that afternoon, it just happened. I was sitting outside with a blanket around me, drinking a cup of coffee and looking at the horizon. My gaze was drawn to some bright flashes of light particles up above my head, and a strong vision came to mind. Suddenly, I saw myself from the outside. I saw John as a tiny little figure in very spacious surroundings. He seemed alone. Then the question came to mind, *If John is down there, alone, and I am up here, who am I?*

All of a sudden, I understood: *I am really not John. John is within the realm of something much bigger, and that larger realm is the real me, outside of my John personality. I'm something bigger than that.*

As I thought this, I was having the most magical feeling inside that I've ever had—totally quiet, just like when a jet first breaks the sound barrier. An absolute silence, both on the inside and outside. A recurring fear I had long had—of not being able to manage things well—disappeared, and it has never returned.

That afternoon was when the phrase "connected resonance" first came to me. I was resonating with a larger realm, a realm that was connecting me with everything. It was a part of everything, and it allowed me to be a part of everything, too. "Connected resonance" is the only phrase that seems to capture the knowledge I gained that day.

My birthday is February 22, but November 28, 2013, is my second birthday. I began a new life that day with a very strong soul connection that allowed me to resonate with my real self.

Now here I am, telling you my story, and you might think, *Yeah, yeah, good for him. But this is certainly not how it looks in my life, and nobody is coming to my rescue.*

I almost couldn't believe it either, but still it happened. And I'm sure it can happen for you, too. If you want it to happen—a lot!—it will happen. And it's something everyone should want a lot. Because whatever you can achieve and accomplish in life on the outside is great, but unless you have a strong connection inward with your higher self, you will never be totally satisfied with life. The cravings to have more, do more, be more and accomplish more will plague you. But if you can uncover the connected resonance with all creation that's always available within you, you'll realize that you're not a human doing—you're a human being. And while doing is a state of activity, being is a state of fullness, completion and wholeness.

This deep insight changed me. I have learned that two things will set us free: our awareness of our judgmental thought patterns and our willingness and guts to face the fear within. It takes a lot of patience and determination to develop these two things. It took me almost two decades to get to the point of setting myself free from my negative thought patterns. It has been a very tough fight with a very strong opponent, the ego. I have been challenged continuously to go outside my comfort zone to find the point of silence within.

Why? Because the ego never lets you rest. It's the strong judging force within your thinking pattern that rules you and creates your fears: the fear of not having a family, not having a job or not having money, or the fear of people not acknowledging you, caring about you and socializing with you. The fear of not feeling special. But if you keep facing these fears and seeing them as the manipulative work of the ego, not as anything real, they can lose their grip on you. They can become less real and easier to brush away.

Let me ask you a question. If you weren't seduced by your ego to feel fear and instead lived in a state of complete fearlessness, what would that mean for your life? And what if that were true for others as well: your family, your society or even the world at large? What a remarkable world this could be if we all acted out of our inner experience of connected resonance rather than out of fear.

As many spiritual teachers have said, we are in this world but not of it. We come here being no thing, no body, then we become "somebody" and go on to become no body again when we leave. Who gave us the suggestion to suddenly become "somebody" if it wasn't the ego?

My ego used to run me. My personal identification with my name and social security number, and my identification with my family, friends and social relations was what meant the most to me. But I had to give up that attachment to, and identification with, the outside world and connect instead with the realm inside of me. I had to find my true identity as the unbounded soul within my bodily presence in the world. And through it all, the most difficult task was being all alone fighting the judgmental "dragon" of my ego. But the struggle was worth it. There's freedom on the other side of that fight. I've learned much and had many insights since November 28, so I no longer just believe—I now *know* that there is a force within each and every one of us that guides us and leads us by example. If you're willing to follow that deeper wisdom, instead of trusting the ego, you too will get to know the truth that brings liberation from the ego-driven life that makes us all miserable.

I assure you, your relationships with others will benefit from the internal resonance and soul connection you gain. Your identity becomes more balanced as you resonate with your deeper self, and you automatically live and act from a more balanced state. Instead of projecting fears or judgmental issues onto others, you'll be projecting love and acceptance. With the soul in the driver's seat instead of the ego, problems seem to disappear.

I no longer consider myself to be living in service of the ego but in service of the soul. I believe we can all take the journey to a freedom within that is beyond the ego, beyond the seen, in the field of infinite possibilities.

Let me offer a few suggestions on how you can make quick progress on your journey to a state of connected resonance with your soul:

1. Each morning when you wake up, say, "Thank you very much for this wonderful day!" to acknowledge and celebrate that you've been given another day and another opportunity to experience freedom and awakening. This is the exercise of thankfulness.

2. Ask yourself, "What can I do for my higher self today that will bring me the energy and bliss that will make this day the best it can be?" This exercise will help you keep your higher self in mind every day.

3. Meditate for at least 15 minutes every day to free your mind of thinking and stress-related issues, and to create new patterns of connecting deep within. Meditation is a proven tool for getting into a relaxed state and out of negative thinking.

4. Create positive affirmations, like "I am feeling good; I am happy within"—small sentences that you can say to yourself inwardly as mantras. Combine this with a body posture that matches what you say: shoulders back, head high. Do this when you go for a walk, cook your meals or pause from activity during the day. This exercise trains your brain to cope with and accept new patterns of behavior and at the same time disconnect from negative thought patterns.

5. When you go to bed each night, say, "Thank you for this day," then rewind and play the mental video of your top three positive experiences of the day, and visualize the positive things you want to see coming up the next day. Positive visualizations at bedtime

strengthen your brain's ability to work unconsciously and process the information while you sleep.

There may be lots of reasons not to start this journey of liberation—or at least, your ego and your fears may try to convince you of that. On the other hand, if you take the journey and experience your own connected resonance with the unbounded part of yourself (your soul), you will create a life of fullness beyond your dreams. There's a freedom within you that you need to experience before you leave this earthly plane. I urge you to seek it now. Why wait?

John Tolmie is a Danish NLP (neuro-linquistic programming) master trainer, a master coach and an inspirational life mentor, who lives in Norway. The father of two children from a previous marriage, he lives with his partner, Solveig Rådahl, with whom he runs their company, Ethos Academy. John coaches students to combine the tools and skills of communication and deep change work with a personal journey to deep inner awareness and insights. One of the most experienced NLP coaches in all of Scandinavia, he has had more than 9,000 client sessions to date. John has also developed several NLP techniques and Connected Resonance®, a course that will grow your inner wisdom. For more information and inspiration, and to receive your free gift, please visit his website, www.johntolmie.com.

Chapter 23

How to Survive the Unsurvivable

Kirsten Stendevad

I had spent nine years working with women, helping them make their wildest dreams come true, when I faced my own worst nightmare: my middle son was diagnosed with a rare form of cancer. Everything I believed in was suddenly put to the test.

If you're facing or have faced catastrophe in your own life, then I know you'll be able to relate and hopefully be reminded of our ability to go up instead of down, no matter what.

It was just before Christmas: December 23, 2011. My husband, Esben, had gone to the hospital with Sebastian, our six-year-old, for the fourth time in the past week to find out why he had a sore chest. When I took Esben's place at 3:00 PM, I looked into the sterile hospital room and saw my child lying in a giant scanning machine with just his little face showing.

When the doctor came out, I could tell something was terribly wrong.

"Is it serious?" I asked. And then it suddenly burst out of me: "Is it cancer?"

Her eyes were dark with pain. "Yes."

My world crumbled.

Fifty women had just passed their final exam at my International Feminine Leadership Academy (IFLA) certification training. I'd taught them how to create positive transformation for themselves and others. Now it was my turn to test my beliefs. Could I create positive transformation for myself and my family in this seemingly impossible situation?

I looked at my beloved boy and for a moment only saw his absence. How could this be? *My* baby? The one who was born on Valentine's Day and always left flowers for me on my keyboard? Sebastian was a healthy, spirited boy who was smart and popular in school and charmed everyone with his curly golden hair and naughty, freckled smile. Esben and I had done everything we could to create a healthy child, as we also did with Sebastian's two brothers. We had performed sacred cleansing rituals prior to conception and raised him on health food and preventive healing techniques, including those to neutralize negative thoughts and feelings.

Yet here I was in the Children's Cancer Unit at the general hospital in Copenhagen with tears running down my cheeks. Approximately 100 children a year get cancer in Denmark. There is almost no chance of getting the rare cancer my son had. One would have to work with asbestos for 30 years *and* be exceptionally unfortunate to contract this type of cancer.

I wondered, *Are we random victims of life's injustice or have we done something wrong?* Since no one can know what is true, I chose a story that strengthened me: this is happening for us to find innovative cancer cures for the benefit of all.

I knew I'd have to use all of the knowledge, faith and wisdom I had acquired thus far in life to get through this crisis. I began to think of the principles I taught in my feminine leadership training in a different light. They were now lifelines we would need in this perilous time, starting with the first one:

Principle #1: Don't Be a Victim! Find Solutions by Balancing Yin and Yang

One of the pillars of my teaching is that women must liberate themselves from the role of victim that we all too often adopt. We can improve both our own world and the world at large by taking a leadership role in exploring new ways to create balance in our lives.

I've come to believe that success, and health, are achieved by balancing yin and yang, feminine and masculine. The common cancer treatments—chemotherapy, surgery and radiation—use only yang, the masculine energy. This is the rational, action-oriented paradigm, which only considers the external factors, so those who survive these treatments often do so with lasting harm. I had to balance yang with yin, the feminine essence, which is about wholeness and the internal aspect of life.

We decided that, since chemo and other yang cancer treatments work *against* the body, they must be complemented with a holistic regimen that works *with* the body and addresses the emotional, spiritual and energetic levels of life. So we brought in lots of alternative, holistic healing modalities, as well as soul-feeding music, games, delicious health foods and toys: anything that would uplift and delight Sebastian.

Meanwhile, my husband and I looked at all areas of our family life, asking, *Where can we create more balance?* We evaluated our marriage, work habits, exercise habits, diet and ways of thinking and feeling, taking our cue from the IFLA philosophy that we thrive best if we nurture all areas of life and live a life in tune with our inner core.

We felt we made progress; however, we soon met a fundamental challenge: the doctors could not find a clear diagnosis and treatment for Sebastian. After 14 days, despite healing help from holistic experts near and far, the tumor had grown by 50 percent. It was too large for radiation and positioned in a manner that prevented surgery.

"Two more weeks, and he cannot breathe," the doctor said, so we had to start the chemotherapy, even though they still didn't even know the cancer's name.

We had to bring in the second principle.

Principle #2: Pleasure and a Constructive Mindset Are Crucial for Health and Success

This key concept of the IFLA concerns the importance of pleasure and positivity, in part because they increase the yin aspect, which is where the body's self-healing processes take place. I knew we needed to do everything we could to support our vision for a positive outcome, so while Sebastian was having chemo with four of the most toxic substances in the world seeping into his blood, I made him laugh and told him stories about the magical drops that could dissolve the "sour cells." There were only two options: crumble under the weight of powerlessness—or stop judging and focus on creating a joyful, lighthearted atmosphere. I chose the latter.

Sebastian himself was our greatest role model. One minute he could be sad or angry that it hurt to take a blood test, but the next moment he might be talking about a nice igloo he had built when he was in kindergarten or a strange name he had heard in the school yard. His delight in little things showed me the way to go. We sat together playing Smurf games; I massaged his feet; we slept in the same bed. If happiness in the Now could help with his healing, these moments of pure joy should work wonders.

Family and friends came swarming with mountains of packages and entertaining company. I brought in a pink yoga mat for the hospital room. Because self-care is one of the key concepts of my Feminine Leadership Academy I also took a day trip to London to have a change of air and a soothing facial.

Immediately after the first round of chemo was over, I flew Sebastian to one of the best holistic cancer hospitals in Germany.

"*Mein Gott,* he is so poisoned," said the chief doctor. But he was able to remove most of the side effects of the chemo without the use of traditional medicine.

In spite of this success, the German doctors felt that Sebastian's disease was seriously malignant, and they did not dare to take responsibility for his treatment. And so we returned to Copenhagen and focused on the next principle.

Principle #3: Go for Your Vision—Even If It Looks Impossible

On January 27, just over a month after Sebastian's first diagnosis of cancer, the Danish doctors finally identified it as a rare, highly aggressive pleural form of cancer, never before seen, worldwide, in a child. Chemotherapy might slow the growth, but only for a short while. Survival chance: zero. Our only hope: find a miracle. "Miracles are my specialty," I insisted and refused anything less.

Loving networks of women helping each other to live their dreams has always been the hallmark of the IFLA. Through this network we gained access to the best cancer doctors, international healers, alternative centers and innovative healing paths around the globe. Of these professionals, 99 percent said they couldn't save him, but 1 percent of them were willing to try. I flew him to Rome, Geneva and Brussels to see experts, and we imported Japanese fungal medicine, Chinese Chi-Lel, Australian heat therapy and much more.

And all the traveling and experimenting with alternatives seemed to pay off: Sebastian was able to stop taking all pain medications, and outwardly he seemed 100 percent well! We thought he was finally on the mend.

On February 14, Sebastian Calvin Kenzo turned seven, and we celebrated his birthday five times. Could this be his last birthday? Was he really getting well or was his good state a respite—a gift from God, so we could remember him as happy and healthy? We did not know, but we focused on our vision: curing the incurable.

It was a special time. Sebastian enjoyed himself with his family and friends and even made much progress with his reading and writing. One day he came home from a visit with his grandparents with a bracelet made of heart-shaped beads and a ring of stars. He told me, "I have made this for you, and I have filled it with love, so you'll never get sick."

On March 14, 2012, we were told he was in top condition, an exceptional patient with no side effects from the chemo he was continuing to receive. The chief doctor at the hospital said, "Whatever you're doing, it works!" The only problem: the tumor was still 100 percent intact.

We continued with our alternative therapies and chose to keep our firm belief that it was possible for him to heal, and Sebastian continued to improve. After a while, he got so strong we were even able to send him back to school! He had some wonderful days with his classmates.

But then the nightmare began—his symptoms returned. The doctors saw this as a "progression of the disease." Our holistic experts argued that we were witnessing a "healing crisis" where symptoms worsen before they disappear. I clung to my vision with every cell—I could not afford to deviate from it. But on May 14, the Danish doctor told us Sebastian had only a few weeks left.

"Not in my world," I replied and flew his weak little body to Austria for yet another cutting-edge cancer treatment.

I carried him around everywhere. We whispered declarations of love to each other. "I will never move away from home," he promised me and kissed my cheek, a kiss simultaneously so deep yet feather-light.

"I cannot help thinking about the fact that I shall die," he said one day, out of the blue. My legs were shaking.

Sebastian transformed from child to sage. He was stoic, uncomplaining and heroic. He patiently bore all the pain and indignities, while our cadre of therapists, healers and doctors worked night and day to heal him. During this time we tried to fulfill his every desire and fill every second with love, as all five of us lived together in a large hotel room in Austria. At the IFLA, we aspire to live our greatest selves, and I felt that my son invited the whole family to step up to that highest level.

On June 11, Sebastian took a turn for the worse. The doctors advised us to call his older brother and the grandparents so they could say good-bye. His family and healers gathered around him to do whatever they could. It was a room full of heavy hearts—and of endless, unconditional love.

On June 12, 2012, Sebastian lay in the arms of his mother and father through the night. His older brother slept with a hand on his shoulder. I wondered if our brave little superhero perceived everything we whispered to him to support him on his journey. For my part, I witnessed the same primordial force as when he was born: metamorphosis.

As the sun cast its first orange rays across the rooftops, his breathing became slower. Then even slower. Then our beloved Sebastian Calvin Kenzo became silent and lay completely still. We covered him with soft kisses as long as his little body was warm.

So, did I realize my vision with pleasure, as I teach other women to do? Did the principles of the IFLA work? In many ways, yes. I furthered the work to find the cure for cancer, as we tried alternative methods that complement the traditional ones and experienced how the two systems can work together. I also managed to create a loving six months of farewell for the whole family, from which we all grew.

But I did not fulfill my deepest desire to keep my son alive.

Does this mean that I failed my exam? To answer this, I have had to resort to external examiners. I have asked a number of gurus and spiritual masters, including the holy lamas in Tibet.

The answer goes something like this: although we are creators, we are also created. A soul comes with a particular mission, and when it is lived out, it travels back to light again. Souls do not think in terms of time. And they ally themselves in advance with the soul groups that can help them with their mission. I am told: "You cannot stop a soul who is scheduled to go back. He chose to come to you because of your spiritual mind. He stayed as long as he could because he loved you so much."

Perhaps the biggest lesson I learned is that I have more access to feminine power when I am open and receptive to the flow of life, than when I am resisting it. I thought I would die if my child died. But to my surprise I continued to breathe, even as I laid his body in the coffin, said good-bye in front of 200 people in the church and saw his small coffin be lowered into the ground.

I knew I had to keep using the IFLA principles, this time to determine whether my life would become better or worse from here. Sometimes I have howled like a she-wolf in the moonlight because Hell is only a thought away. But so is gratitude that Sebastian was ever here with us. I am also grateful for the countless new openings of my heart, mind and spirit that I have gained by facing the immense pain. I imagine that my son is in Paradise, and I choose to create Heaven on Earth now, as my other children deserve a happy mother.

I can focus on what I am missing or on what I am receiving, like the experience of communicating, even now, with his beautiful soul. Many of the tools I teach continue to help, such as the practices that allow me to let the emotions run through me, instead of creating blocks.

I miss my son on Earth, but I feel truly blessed to experience his everlasting presence in my heart. Something in me understands that, as long as we love, it is not possible to lose.

Kirsten Stendevad, CEO of Illumina International, is an expert in 21ˢᵗ-century leadership paradigms, which she has been teaching leaders with and without titles since 2003. The co-author of five trendsetting bestsellers about innovative and visionary leadership, she has also given workshops on these topics at Harvard Business School, MIT and McKinsey & Co., among others.

Kirsten is well-known among the creative class as a transformative role model, a community leader and an inspiring mentor, not least for female changemakers and entrepreneurs. Her latest business book, The Future is Feminine, *will soon be available in English. Also trained as a kundalini yoga teacher and evolutionary coach, Kirsten lives in Copenhagen, Denmark, with her husband and three sons, two on Earth and one in Heaven. She has been greatly helped by her eldest son's book,* How to Have an Invisible Brother, *available at davidcozmo.com. You can reach Kirsten at www.kirstenstendevad.com.*

——— *Chapter 24* ———

Picking Up the Pieces:
How to Find Wholeness Through Journaling

Dr. Markeita L. Banya

J anuary 2005

Tick Tock. Tick Tock. The sound seemed to be getting louder and louder, like a bass drum approaching in the annual holiday parade.

It had been midnight in my life for longer than I cared to remember. Mornings were a reminder and a reflection of my deepest fear. Here I was, sitting on the bed, wishing the comforter could live up to its name. *Hold me tight and never let me go!*

In a matter of seven days, the fortress called my life had come crumbling down, and all the king's men could not put it back together again. All gone: Adolescent kids. Big house. New car. Brand-name clothes. Potential husband. Longtime friends. Growing business. Bank account. Promising career.

You are probably asking yourself. *What happened to her? Was she addicted to drugs? Pain medications? How did she lose everything?*

You got it. It was all due to self-medicating getting out of hand. I had lost everything.

I could no longer hide. Everyone was going to know that I was indeed inadequate to have and hold on to anything deemed worthy in this world. Even my sanity seemed to elude me as the ticking got louder in my mind. Here I was in this extended-stay hotel room, looking at myself with no mirror in sight. Was I dying? Had Life traded me in and dropped me off at Death's door? My life movie was playing at warp speed and nothing seemed to be right.

Why was I going through this? I had been going to church all my life. Heck, all I *knew* was Jesus. The ticking seemed to come to a loud roar when I whispered, "Jesus."

I was too ashamed to ask Him for help.

And then the sky got darker. The cycle of teen motherhood that had been my fate would continue with my daughter. In a scan at the OB clinic, a 26-week-old male fetus appeared on the screen. Disappointment. Anger. Fear. All welled up as I tried to hold myself together so I could be there for my daughter. The statistics for teen moms that I'd fought so hard to bring down were growing right here in my daughter's belly.

But it was the discovery of who the father was that sent shock waves through our family and challenged my very being. No type of medication and no consoling words could stop my worst nightmare turned reality, nor could I speak about what my eyes witnessed and my ears heard. While it's tempting to say incest is most common in a certain demographic, it's not true. Incest happens in every type of family. It happened in my family. And the guilt of not having known about it was torture for me.

In the weeks to come, the once-blue skies of my life remained blackened by this heartache—and all the other ongoing issues: no money, countless court dates, disgruntled employees, disheartened clients, broken friendships, homelessness and a growing hole in my heart. Though, truth be told, the hole had been there for most of my life. I had tried to fill it up with everything from alcohol and sex to education, a career and my relationship with God Himself.

But the hole remained ever-present, and now the world would know what I had known for most of my life: I was scared and I had no place to go. I had no energy to run or fight.

The only solution would be to surrender. Didn't I surrender when I got baptized, not once but twice? Didn't I surrender when I decided to fly my children to their father, with the possibility of never seeing them again? Didn't I surrender when I sold everything that was not destroyed in the flooded basement, or repossessed? Didn't I surrender when I said that I would feel the pain regardless of how much I wanted to medicate it from this day forward?

In the midst of the raging thoughts of surrender, the ticking clock became a quiet hum, and I was beginning to breathe.

And then I heard it. A whisper of gentleness: "You have not given Me your heart." Tears fell. It was the first time in nearly two decades that I had felt anything, let alone shed a tear. It was true. I wanted to surrender my heart to the Lord, but I couldn't find the way. I was so broken; why would He want me?

I had been screaming for years to be free, but now I knew that what I really wanted was to be whole. I was in pieces, and peace was nowhere to be found. How could I find it? Wholeness and peace seemed to be synonymous for me. I had asked for it each year for the past 10 Christmases. It seemed to be a gift no one, including God and myself, was able to give me. I had subscribed to the belief that life was hard and peace would come with death when I walked the streets of Heaven. I had believed what I was told for so many years as a child.

How do you know when you're at a turning point in your life? When the pain you're feeling truly becomes unbearable. It is your turning point that gives you the motivation to put on your big-girl panties and do what you need to do. Treatment of pain is the foundation of our healthcare system, so you and I have learned at an early age to medicate pain. Take an aspirin if it hurts. But self-medication is a slippery slope.

As a medical professional, I agree that you should seek medical care when you're experiencing pain, whether emotional or physical. But I caution you to take a second look. If your body has begun to shut down with dis-ease, or you've gotten to a point where you know that you can't keep living the way you have until now, often these pains are signs that you need to make a significant change in your life, whether it's a spiritual change or a very practical, everyday-life change.

Change is hard—but essential. Most often, peace and wholeness come only when you are ready and willing to make some major changes in your life. The first step begins with identifying your core beliefs. If you do not identify these core beliefs, you will find yourself shortchanging yourself by cutting corners with your emotional issues, like putting fingernail polish on a run in your pantyhose instead of throwing them in the trash and buying a new pair, or going without.

Peace and wholeness come from knowing your core beliefs, which are found at the core of your authentic self. But you'll never experience them unless you're in touch with that core. Why not try a simple exercise to help you discover your authentic self and maybe improve your relationships or even transform your life? I call it "Spiritual Journaling: Writing Your Own Internal Story."

I discovered the gift of journaling when I was deep in the darkest part of my own transformation process. And over time I found it was a way to "clear my path." It helped me see where I was and where I might be headed. Most importantly, it helped me see what I truly wanted in life.

Journaling gives you an opportunity to see through a different lens. As your authentic self comes forth onto the page, you become increasingly aware of how you create your own reality. After you've done it for a while, I think you'll look at your thoughts, ideas, emotions and beliefs, and then see how they're influencing and even creating the reality you're experiencing.

Now, you might say you've journaled before and it wasn't that significant or helpful in your life. It's true that, without training our minds to see the impact of certain beliefs we're hanging on to, journaling could seem unimportant. But I believe that putting pen to paper is one of the most powerful tools we have in life. Scientific research supports the concept that writing about stressful events helps you come to terms with them, thus reducing their impact on your physical health. While your left brain is analyzing and rationalizing, your right brain is free to create and to feel. As a result, writing lessens the pain and also lets you use all of your brainpower to better understand yourself, others and the world around you.

It's common in many cultures for young girls to begin writing their secrets in their diaries. But I was not the typical little girl who kept a diary. The closest I came to journaling was writing poetry. My poetic license was cut short as a teen, though, when a respected adult deemed my poetry vulgar. So, I had a serious attitude problem when, years later, the social worker for my children had the nerve to suggest I try journaling. I thought, *The last time I shared myself on paper, it was not accepted. What's it going to do for me and my kids now?* But it turned out that this was my turning point: I couldn't medicate the pain anymore, and journaling proved to be exactly the support I needed.

My first guide was Katherine Revoir, whose book *Spiritual Doodles and Mental Leapfrogs* teaches you firsthand how to write in a way that uses both the right and left sides of your brain, while also awakening your heart. Right away, I found that journaling opened my heart and let me connect with the Divine in an easy and genuine way. My first journal began as an all-out complaining session about my entire life, which almost sounded like a familiar prayer. Then somewhere along the way, the writing shifted to self-awareness and spiritual revelation. My pain had found its release and its purpose.

I really like the saying, "You cannot conquer what you are not willing to confront." And my favorite form of confrontation is through the written word. I urge you to try it out.

Here are some easy steps to get started:

1. Grab a notebook or blank sheets of paper and find a pen or pencil, or maybe a set of colored pencils for more fun. You can purchase a fancy diary or just use the Notes app on your phone.
2. A common place to start with journaling is writing your thoughts immediately as they come to your mind. But I suggest you try this: Without thinking too much or worrying about what to write about, just write until you feel empty. You can begin with what today was like or with an angry response to something that's bothering you, like I did when I started a journal entry with "I know this lady did not just tell me…" The important thing is just to write whatever comes up and keep it up for a few days or a few weeks.

3. There's no time frame and no right or wrong. No one is grading your paper. No points are taken off for misspelled words, poor grammar or writing outside the lines or even drawing pictures. Feel free to express yourself in all ways in your journaling. The only requirement is that you *do not read* as you go along. Do not try to control your writing; just let it flow. Allow your heart to explore. Let the words peel back the layers of your soul.

4. When you have gotten to an empty place, simply stop. Don't fret. You will know the empty place. It's where you have said all you can say about that. You can take a break of a few days to a week, or you can keep writing on another topic. One word of caution about stopping: avoid taking a break when you've been writing about a sensitive or difficult part of your life. If you're stopping because it hurts, it's better to just allow the pain to push you through the tears and snot, and continue to write.

5. When you return to your journal after some time away and read what you wrote, you might be able to unwrap your thoughts and feelings more. The delay provides a shift in perspective that lets you see your life from a different point of view. You might see something for the first time, maybe a belief you've been holding unconsciously that isn't true or helpful. Seeing it can break the hypnotic effect the belief had on you. Now, you can see the truth and be free of it.

As you read, jot down the repetitive thoughts, recurring ideas and unfulfilled desires you expressed. Then, with fresh eyes, continue journaling about these discoveries. Now you can go a little deeper to discover more about your unconscious beliefs and how they have affected your relationships and your life. If you need help, check out "core belief inventory" online for much more about how to uncover your unconscious beliefs.

Journaling took me from being broken into a million little pieces to being a whole and happy human being. I went from struggling to hold my life together to becoming the author of my own success story. Journaling even led me to have better relationships, which can only show up when you've got your own life together. I have been willing to confront—and able to conquer—so much that held me back in the past. And I wish the same for you. I am very happy and excited for you, as you begin to use this tool to unwrap *your* precious gifts of peace, happiness and wholeness.

Fueled by a desire to serve, Rev. Dr. Markeita L. Banya has worked tirelessly to expand her knowledge base and expertise in the field of medical aesthetics and wellness as an anti-aging clinician. She pens each face with a personal, age-appropriate signature of vitality and beauty. Today, she has taken a handful of her personal life stories from her four marriages, a dash of spiritual revelation and a pinch of scientific principles to create works in print and on the international stage. Dr. Markeita's naked truth is a real-life recipe for a woman experiencing love and life. Check out her website, www. DrMarkeita.com, for upcoming events and her new books, A Divorcee's Do-Over: Tips, Tools and Techniques for a Complete Self-Love and Forgiveness Makeover *and* A Sexy Do-Over: Tips, Tricks and Toys for Great Sex and Intimacy.

Chapter 25
Live Life from Your Joy Center!
Lisa McDonald

I was four years old and not a happy girl. I did not like my step-grandfather, Reg. I didn't trust him, and I had ample reason to fear him. Always the first to volunteer to tuck me in with a bedtime story, Reg used me to fulfill his sexual needs, ensuring that it was him, not me, who would have a good night's sleep. The bedtime-story routine was a nightmare from which I couldn't wake up. Reg had carte blanche to take me to shops and shower me with shut-up tokens, which I knew were simply bribes to keep my mouth shut. Thus, objects as innocent as a stuffed animal or a bag of sweets embedded shame and self-loathing deep in my heart and mind.

Reg's abuse created deep wounds, but today I'm a successful author, radio show host and mother of two beautiful children. The following is my story, but it can also be your story, no matter what you've been through or had to endure. I hope that hearing my story and the steps I took to change my life can help you emerge into a new life, as well.

For many years, my adult life was colored by those six years of sexual abuse. For much of that time, I felt semi-paralyzed in a cloud of PTSD-induced

184

confusion. I had one foot caught in a mire of fear, while the other tried to race ahead. I yearned to be victorious and wave the warrior-spirit banner for all the world to see. But part of me was stuck in a dark, sad place.

The ping-pong game of wins and losses between the two facets of myself was an exhausting struggle. There was the Lisa who approached life, relationships and opportunities paralyzed by a fear of when the next shoe would drop, and the Lisa who worked twice as hard as everyone else to reach the finish line. I never knew which version of myself was going to show up during the various stages and milestones of my life. I just knew, very early on in my journey, that my life would *not* be defined by what had happened to me at the defenseless age of four. That was nonnegotiable.

Fast-forward to another personal crisis at 40 years of age. That's when I joined the 50 percent of the population who are single parents and/or divorced. Old wounds from my fractured family resurfaced as my marriage ended. Knowing the pain and confusion I felt when my birth family fell apart, I was fiercely intent on that never becoming my children's reality.

I'd been working intimately with families for 25 years at this point, as a member of senior management in social services, especially crisis management. It had been my role to empower, educate and advocate for individuals and families in crisis, so I couldn't turn a blind eye to the unhealthiness of my own marriage and its downward spiral into crisis. When I looked in the mirror or at my children's innocent faces, I saw the damage it was doing and could feel it inside myself, as well. There was no escaping the trouble that lay ahead for all of us if I didn't take the hard step of ending the marriage.

So, I moved with my two children back to my home province in Canada with the intention of rebuilding from the ground up. I was frightened. I felt isolated. This step just seemed unimaginable for me, as I had no clear sense of direction.

My children were only three years and 18 months old. Their daddy accepted a three-year engineering contract in Madagascar, Africa—a six-weeks-out, 10-days-back rotation. Co-parenting on this schedule proved unhealthy, so I faced a different form of personal hell when he was with us every six weeks. After a while, I moved into a hotel when he came, so he could bond and play catch-up with our children. They pleaded with me not to leave them, for I was their security blanket and we had already endured so much loss and change. Unfortunately, letting him be with them for those 10 days at a time was the best solution I could come up with in a gut-wrenching situation. And yes, we did overcome it and survive it, although there were many occasions where, emotionally and spiritually, I didn't believe I could or would.

When my youngest started full-time school, I had to face the next big hurdle. How will I earn money to support myself and my children? Now, I was struck with another kind of paralysis. I knew it wasn't an option to return to my previous job, as I needed to be accessible and available to my children as their primary caregiver, and my old job wouldn't allow that. There were so many nights when I put Quinn and Olivia to bed, then pushed myself to sit up late and try to figure out a sustainable plan for the three of us. How was I going to hold on to this new house? How would I pay the never-ending bills? How could I instill a genuine sense of stability and security in my children, mostly on my own?

I felt like I was falling into an abyss. Yet, in spite of those feelings, I had to figure out the answers to these crucial, time-crunched questions. I can't tell you how many times I cried and pleaded and prayed for Universal Guidance. I lacked direction, vision and clarity, and felt lost. In my darkest moments, I envisioned homelessness and the three of us huddling together in a shelter. I had been the director of several women and children's shelters! How in the world did I wind up here?

Gradually, the Universal Guidance I pleaded and prayed for began to appear. First, I got the idea that I wanted to find what I called "the Joy Center" inside myself. I knew there must be a place of joy somewhere inside of me, because there had been times when I had experienced joy in the past. If I could just find and connect with that, I knew my life would begin to change.

To do that, I knew I had to completely change the movie reel running in my head and replace the negativity and fear that had been overwhelming me with nonnegotiable positivity and manifestation. So I tried different things. I began writing down everything I aspired to accomplish or reverse in my life. I began reading inspirational stories wherever I could find them. I began looking in the mirror every day and reciting heartfelt, self-supporting affirmations, such as "I have the power to create a life I love" and "All the love I give comes back to me a thousand-fold." Essentially, I chose to deliberately love myself, on purpose, no matter the circumstances.

Little by little, these practices transformed me into a woman on a mission with a completely new lease on life. The core of who I have always known myself to be finally came through, out of darkness and out of necessity. Thank God! I began to revel in gratitude daily and to love and appreciate everything and everyone. I looked for and found tremendous gifts in all the heartache, the struggle, the inner conflict, the confusion, the tears, and the sleepless nights and days of fog and fatigue. As that happened, I began to feel grateful for everything I'd been through because it allowed me to recreate my life.

And then I had the idea to write a children's book. So I did. And then I wrote another. Mentally, I never questioned it. I just committed myself to the process of fumbling my way through it, one step at a time. I submitted the books to a publisher and they were both published! Next, I was blessed to find myself paired with a successful and highly respected publicist, who continues to enhance my career and work his magic behind the scenes to this day. And the books flew off the shelves! Those two books continue to sell well at various Canadian bookstores and through Toys "R" Us.

I knew that, by focusing on gratitude and on the good in my life, I'd created a new way of living, and that had sparked the idea of writing these books, which in turn allowed me to find my amazing publicist. I also knew that, to keep this going, I would have to continue to work on my thinking and my way of being with this level of success. I would have to *really* stay in touch with my Joy Center. So I developed habits of positive thinking and living and practiced them seriously. I thought about what gives me joy and immersed myself in positive, inspiring books. I visualized my ongoing success and found people who would support me in achieving it. And I kept the gratitude flowing.

When I embraced with wholehearted gratitude the totality of my journey to date, a wonderful thing happened: I discovered what it is to unconditionally love myself. I had not only reinvented my life; I had, more importantly, reinvented a stronger, healthier and clearer version of myself. I was, once and for all, Lisa, not defined by life circumstances; Lisa, not defined by heartache and strife. I was curious, fearless, navigating my way from a place of love and gratitude. I sponged up everything good before me and chose to recognize and embrace the lessons on how to transform darkness into light.

And the results kept coming in my life. I began to attend biweekly book signings and host my own weekly radio show and collaborate with many well-known people within the publishing industry. I also wrote a third and fourth book in the series, which are currently being illustrated and will soon be sent off to the printer. Next, I look forward to moving on to writing for adults in the transformational and personal development genre.

The list of potential projects is endless, and, truly, these days I feel like the sky's the limit. The clearer I get in my goals and my sense of self, the more aligned I become with quality and the more I have found myself in the company of like-minded, brightly lit and passionate souls. Every single day I'm choosing to take major action steps in my life. What's on my to-do list today would have been on my maybe-someday list a few years ago.

There's every reason why my story can also be your story. You have a Joy Center in you, just as I do. You have unique gifts and talents to discover, just as I did. All that's required is to decide it's time for your life to change and then to start taking action. Begin with the following seven steps that helped me transform my life, and then prepare for miracles.

Step #1: Soak up as much positivity and inspiration as you can.

I turned to books (including *The Passion Test*), quotes, meditation, YouTube videos, inspirational people, volunteering, journaling and spending time being present with nature.

Step #2: Take action on a daily basis to become clear on what your Joy Center is and then act on that discovery.

Make an unwavering commitment to achieve at least one forward-thinking, tangible win for yourself every day. For me, this commitment rapidly gained momentum and led to a succession of daily wins in all areas of my life, including furthering my career as a writer and speaker, creating more cooperative family relationships and establishing a better-structured home life.

Step #3: Make a pact with yourself that it's nonnegotiable to love yourself unconditionally.

I upheld this pact by taking time every day, no matter what challenges or temporary setbacks were present, to look in the mirror and lovingly offer my reflections, self-proclamations, I-statements, praise and appreciation of my ongoing resilience, tenacity and fortitude. I took myself under my own wing and began nurturing myself in a way no one else in my life ever had. It was a huge gift I gave myself, unconditionally and consistently, and a gift you can easily give yourself, as well. Don't let a day pass without looking at yourself in the mirror and saying, "I am a loving, deserving soul who is living a life of abundance."

Step #4: Become a visualizer.

This is a tool I've found to be a very useful barometer for knowing if I'm on the right path. As a result of visualization, I've seen many of my intentions and goals quickly morph into items on my to-do list and then into a finished product, whether books, speaking engagements or peaceful bedtimes for the kids. The lesson in this for me has been that the more clearly I visualize and then pursue the things that give me inner joy and personal fulfillment, the more I grow, expand and improve.

Step #5: Affirm for yourself the importance of acquiring mentors and allowing yourself to be completely receptive to being mentored and coached.

At each step of my journey, I relied on the help of people who had been there before and gotten where I wanted to go. Essentially, I surrendered to experts and "got out of my own way."

Step #6: Express gratitude for everything!

Every morning and throughout the course of each day, I express my deep gratitude for everything: for being gifted with a new day with my children, my health, my family, friends and community; for being able-bodied; for my inner strength; for any gesture of kindness bestowed upon me. The gratitude list remains endless. And I express gratitude frequently when talking with others or posting on social media, when creating marketing and promotional initiatives and most importantly, in my thoughts during times of solitude.

Step #7: Make a commitment to work on yourself every single day.

I challenge myself every day to be the best possible version of myself—to *be* better and to *do* better than the day before. I do this with the awareness that I'm in competition with no one other than myself.

This time of transition has been quite the spiritual emancipation for me as I know it will be for you. I've thanked many for the gentle hands they've graciously extended to me along my journey, and I also wish to thank my own indomitable spirit for not giving up, for not shirking personal responsibility and for not opting to take shortcuts in the long process of reclaiming my most authentic self.

Just as I did, you'll discover so many helping hands along the way. Accept them and be grateful for them. None of us can "do life" on our own. We all need help and support. The journey of personal growth and development is never over, but your commitment to healing and to truly feeling alive will be your biggest accomplishment.

If you want to make progress toward a more fulfilling life but haven't found your way yet, ask yourself, "What's *my* Joy Center?" and try out my seven steps above. As I tuned in to the frequency of my Joy Center, I made the huge discovery of a hidden talent, and I have a feeling you will, too. I am the visionary and the dream—and so are you. I am the teacher and the student—and so are you. Look for your Joy Center and see where it leads you—and what magic happens along the way.

 *Lisa McDonald is a mother, author and TV show host, as well as a radio show host for two global networks, a speaker, a mentor and a life/career coach. Her first two children's books,* Little Boy Gan from Passion-Filled Everland *and* Reimburse the Universe, *show the joy in living a passion-filled life and in giving back. Lisa frequently speaks in schools on topics such as anti-bullying initiatives and the power of leadership when combined with kindness, compassion and being of service to others.*

At the core of Lisa's being is an unwavering commitment to personal growth and to living fearlessly and embracing a yummy-filled life of joy and passions. Lisa loves to connect with others and learn from their stories. Please share your story with her at lisamcdonaldauthor.com or lisamcdonald13@gmail.com. Or contact Lisa via her host pages on radio and TV—ctrnetwork.com, bbmglobalnetwork.com, and 365TVNETWORK.com—and on all social media platforms.

Chapter 26

Up the Emotional Staircase:
Reaching the Wisdom Altitude of Life
Ramon G. Corrales

One day, as I was leaving a parking lot, someone honked and yelled at me, apparently irritated by my being in her way. I felt a sharp stab of anger. As I got in my car and drove off, I felt the anger, welcomed it as my creation and began to listen to it. As is my practice, I asked the anger what message it had for me. The answer was clear: I valued and needed *kindness*, a quality that I viewed as being sadly lacking in the incident, between her yelling and my anger.

I took a few seconds to affirm silently that I am kind person, with the capacity to experience kindness and show it to others. I felt serene again. To reinforce and live this quality, I decided to show kindness to my wife when I got home.

This brief story illustrates a manner of viewing and transforming our emotions in a way that not only changes our *state* of mind but also gradually propels us to a new *stage* of mind, that is, a new mindset we'll carry forward with us. In this chapter I want to share how you can transform every strong feeling in a way that changes both your current state of mind and your ongoing stage of mind.

More recently, I realized a friend of mine had misunderstood what I was saying as a result of not listening carefully, and I felt hurt. I welcomed the feeling as my own and listened to it. The hurt revealed how important being heard and understood are to me. The moment I felt my hurt and heard the message within it, I calmed down. I was able to look at my friend, listen to him intently and make sure I understood him, acting on what I had learned, not on the hurt I had felt.

These experiences illustrate a teaching that I call "A Model for Transforming Emotions" or "Model TE." Let me share the basics with you.

Introducing Model TE

There are four terms that I've found helpful in working with Model TE. An event that disturbs you is a "pebble" that's been thrown into the pond of your self. Pebbles are external to us; they're things we perceive through the five senses. They trigger "ripples" or emotional disturbances within us, but they do not *cause* the ripples (as we'll see later). When the ripples are strong, they become emotional "grenades." On the other hand, the positive qualities that we find within ourselves are "jewels."

To see how the model works, let's assume that a friend said something that triggered anger in you. There are four major steps you can take to use the situation to your advantage:

1. **Feel it.** Feel the anger fully by owning and welcoming it into your heart, mind and body. Take in the feeling, rather than resisting it.
2. **Listen to it.** As you feel the anger, ask yourself: *What is this feeling saying I need?* Maybe you realize you need respect. This is the message from your deeper mind—that respect is important to you. It's one of your jewels.
3. **Affirm the quality in you.** Own it and say to yourself: *I am respectful.*
4. **Commit to act on the message (not on the feeling).** Look at the outside world again. Review the events that led to the words your friend

uttered. Think about the outcome you want from this matter and how you wish to approach it. Visualize your actions and make sure they are respectful. Commit to interacting respectfully with the world.

This is a simple but profound process, and not always easy. When you experience an unpleasant grenade, usually the last thing you want to do is to feel it. But if you do, and you then follow the other three steps, you can convert any experience, however negative, into a positive one.

Practicing this model gradually takes you through three "altitudes" of attitude:

- Starting from the emotional altitude, where you're reacting to your ripples and grenades and guided by the desire for *power*,
- To the principle-based, or strategic, altitude, which involves a rational examination of the facts or events that happened and identifying your ripples and grenades, guided by *principle*, and then
- To acting on your jewels to bring out the best in yourself and others, guided by *purpose*, which is the altitude of wisdom.

A Model for Managing Emotion in Others: A Short Story

Early one Friday morning, I received a call from "Peter," a CEO I coach. He said he was "sick to his stomach with worry about the cash flow" his firm was averaging that week. Peter asked if I could help him "get back on track" emotionally, so he could get into his performance zone again.

Peter had good reason to pay attention to this event. For two weeks in a row, his firm had taken in half of its average revenue of $30,000 to $40,000 per week. This pebble (low revenue) was triggering intense grenades (feeling sick to his stomach).

It would be easy to have compassion for Peter if he succumbed to his inner grenades and became anxious or depressed and lost sleep the rest of the weekend. That is the bottom of the staircase—the emotional altitude. And few of us would object if he called in his leadership team immediately to have a war-room session to address the cash-flow issue strategically. Even if he worried until the cash flow improved, we would praise him for taking action instead of being immobilized by fear. That's the principle-based or strategic altitude of life.

But how much more effective would it be if he could jump to the altitude of wisdom? Peter said his worry revealed his need for success, based on a thirst for excellence. Here's how I helped him apply the Model for Transforming Emotions to meet those needs.

Feel It

ME: Peter, I want you to really welcome that worry as the sick-to-the-stomach feeling, even though you don't like it. It's yours. If this feeling were a child of yours who was suffering, imagine how you would simply be present and accepting, not rejecting.

(A few moments of silence.)

CEO: I can feel it. I accept it. It's mine. It sounds odd to talk this way, but when I stop fighting it, I get it. It's helpful to know I don't have to like the sick-to-my-stomach feeling in order to accept it.

Listen to It

ME: That's good to hear. Now I want you to focus on the success jewel you heard from the grenade of worry. Here's the key: you cannot want something you don't have the capacity to attain, just as you can't feel hunger if you don't have the ability to eat. Your yearning for success—that thirst for excellence—indicates a capacity you have. That is a jewel within you. Affirm it as a quality within. Say to yourself something like: *I have a deep capacity to succeed.*

(A few moments of silence.)

CEO: What if I don't quite believe it?

Affirm the Quality in You

ME: This is why it's important to feel the worry and listen to its message—that success is a deep desire within you, and you wouldn't desire it if you couldn't achieve it. This is what will convince you. It is a deeper sense of knowing, not just an intellectual analysis. Go back and feel the worry and listen to its message again. Let the feeling show you your desire.

(A few moments of silence.)

CEO: I do feel a deep yearning to succeed. And I believe I have the capacity—the ability—to succeed. I thank God for creating this quality in me.

Act on the Jewel

ME: That belief in yourself is the jewel. Now, make a commitment to act on this jewel, not on the grenade of worry. The worry is now simply part of your energy, absorbed and transformed by you, ready to be used in action. But, first, make a jewel-based commitment to act upon your thirst for excellence.

CEO: I get the commitment part, and I'll use that energy to direct my will toward some kind of action. But what do you mean by a "jewel-based commitment"?

ME: This simply means facing every event you encounter with a determination to give it your best, based on your jewel: in this case, your belief in yourself and your ability. As you deal with a customer or co-worker in the course of your day, focus on the task and respond with all the talent and heart you have, free of the blockages of worry and doubt. That's it. That's how you transform the worry into solutions-focused energy, taking you from a state of resistance to one of persistence.

CEO: I get it! The worry itself is not the problem. It carries the message I need to act on in order to generate great solutions.

ME: That's it! Go, face all the pebbles thrown into your pond, and respond with the jewels of determination and commitment that you carry in your soul DNA.

The Rational View Is Necessary But Insufficient

In my view, the rational approach is good but *not good enough*. Why? Because it assumes that the "real" solution is the external change (such as an improvement in cash flow), which isn't under your control. And that puts you into the victim mindset, which is the single greatest stumbling block to developing higher stages of maturity and productivity. If you can learn to be transformational in your approach to life, as in the process above, and own your feelings and transform them, that puts you in the *wisdom seat*.

If you listen to Peter, there is an assumption that the "cause" of the worry is the low cash flow, and therefore the real fix of the worry can occur only when the external results take place. *The belief that the cash flow is the cause of the worry is the poison pill.* It is simply not true, and any solution based on this false assumption will be limited by it.

The Nature of Emotions: The Coded Language of the Soul

For Model TE to be transformative, we need to have a deeper understanding of our feelings:

- **All feelings are good.** Whether pleasant or unpleasant, all our feelings are valuable because they give us important insights into ourselves and the events we encounter. When I felt angry in response to the driver who honked and yelled at me, I discovered how important kindness was to me. I learned something important about myself and what I need to be happy.
- **Use "taking in" vs. "letting go."** I do *not* recommend using language like "let feelings go" or "diminish" or "defuse" them. It's not useful to deny your feelings, and these phrases are simply milder forms of denial. They create a negative relationship between you and your feelings. We need to befriend our feelings and accept them as a part of us, not apart from us. I prefer to use the phrases "let them in" or "take them in."
- **We create our emotions**. We are meaning-makers, feeling-makers and decision-makers. Outside events don't create our inner ripples. *We* create them and any grenades that go off.
- As long as you believe that he, she or it (the world of pebbles) caused your feelings, you'll continue to operate at the egocentric altitude of life based on *power*: you control me or I control you. If you hurt me emotionally, then you need to change your behavior so I can be happy or calm again. We need to change that belief to the following: I can be happy and successful by seeing through my emotions and transforming them.

- **Feelings are informative, not directive.** Although they contain information, feelings do not direct us to act in a particular way. Feelings can provide motivation, but you and I, through an act of will, decide to act in certain ways. Feelings mainly inform us, showing us what we value. My hurt taught me how important understanding is to me, just as my anger showed me how much I value kindness. These messages are the jewels of the soul.

When you are hit by an emotional grenade, such as hurt, you can find the jewel by asking, *What do I need?* The answer reveals not only your need but also a positive quality you possess—that is, a jewel. Look at the following needs and the capacities they potentially reveal:

Your Needs Reveal Your Jewels
- The need for *respect* reveals the capacity to give and receive respect.
- The need for *understanding* reveals the capacity to understand and to be understood.
- The need *to bring value* to others reveals the capacity to contribute to the well-being of others and to receive their contributions.
- The need *to belong or to be included* reveals your capacity to include and to be included.
- The need *to be independent* reveals your capacity for self-directed actions.

So, start your climb up the emotional staircase today. Here are a few practices to get you started. It's an exciting journey that never ends but ever extends.

Beginning Practices for Transforming Emotions
1. Practice Model TE with ripples at work and at home. It helps to start with mild feelings because it's easier to be in charge of them. Intense feelings tend to take over the self quickly. Keep in mind that you are leading the feelings instead of being led by them.
2. Reflect upon events that have triggered grenades within you, and find the jewels in those grenades. Then consider possible jewel-based actions

you could take should similar pebbles strike you again. Compare these actions to the ones you actually took.

3. Identify two grenades you experience at work and two at home. Look at the pebbles that triggered them. Then find the jewels in each of the grenades. Do you see a pattern in the kinds of jewels that emerge? Do you see a pattern in the kinds of pebbles that trigger grenades in you? Take notes and be ready.

4. At the end of the day, review one or two events that affected you, even in a mild way. Accept the events as pebbles meant for you to handle. Then reflect: *If the pebbles are meant for me, the grenades must also be there for me to discover the jewels within my being.* Rest in that awareness. Sleep well.

Every moment can bring a deepening of our relationship to life, from the outer world of pebbles to the interior world of ripples, grenades and jewels. Every action *you* take is also a pebble thrown into the universal pond, affecting other lives. The pebbles you throw carry your unique presence: may they serve the world and bring you many rewards. And may the pebbles that come your way, whether they seem to be good and bad, always help you to grow in wisdom, happiness and success.

Ramon Corrales, PhD, is the CEO of Integral Mastery Center, Inc., and the creator of The Wisdom Code for Personal and Leadership Transformation. Ramon coaches leaders to find the right talent and to manage that talent for high performance, high purpose and high profit. He helps leaders create a culture of productivity and personal development. Ramon's background includes having been a monk, a sociologist, a family therapist and eventually a corporate coach. He brings the depth of human understanding to the importance of high performance at work.

Ramon and his wife, Annabel, have raised two successful daughters and treasure their special relationship with their two grandchildren. Ramon has focused his work on the development of wisdom and its impact on great leadership. Ramon is the author of the book Of Pebbles & Grenades: 3 Keys to Self-Mastery. *He is also a trained NLP practitioner and a certified Kolbe consultant. Follow his work at www. ramoncorrales.coach.*

Chapter 27

Slay Your Giants!
Three Steps to Putting Fear Behind for Good
Dr. Jim Claussen

T he words echoed in my head: "What you think about, you bring about."

Little did I know that the man who was speaking—a chiropractor named Dr. M.T. Morter Jr.—would change my life. I just knew that his words rang true. And I realized that I had already demonstrated the truth of those words in my life, without ever knowing it.

It started one day when I was 22 and decided to completely change the direction of my life. I had been working as an electrician for a few years, but I had bigger dreams. I wanted to make my parents proud—have a family, own a nice car and a big house, and travel. I wanted to live the American dream! I had seen some of the finer things in life when one of my friends was dating a young lady who lived in a 10,000-square-foot house in a gated community. We'd congregate there and hang out in the built-in pool and play tennis on the private courts.

I noticed the license plates there—Dr. This and Dr. That. I thought, *As an electrician, there's no way I'll ever be able to live in a place like this.* But I also thought, *I deserve to have this nicer life! Why not me?* But how was I going to accomplish this?

As fate would have it, I had already been "called into service" five times and just didn't know it. Four years earlier, when I was 18, I dislocated my right shoulder playing football, and my best friend's dad took me to get my first chiropractic adjustment. As I sat in that office, I felt a calling to do more, to be of service to the world in a bigger way, but I didn't listen to it. I continued to play sports and proceeded to dislocate my shoulder five more times. And each time I went to the chiropractor I felt the same calling, and each time I ignored it. I didn't know what to do with it.

After the last, and worst, dislocation, my boss threatened to lay me off work until I was healed. That conversation freaked me out. I was recently engaged and we were planning our future. I had bills and now a wedding to pay for, too. What was I going to do?

Luckily for me, an entrance test for the local electrical union was held that year. There were roughly 1,000 people signed up to take it, but I thought it was worth a shot, even though I'd never been good at test taking. When I received my results, I was shocked to see I was number 58, and they were only taking 60 applicants! I was elated. I was getting into the electrical union!

And then I wasn't. Turned out, there was some quota they had to meet, so I didn't get in. Frustrated and angry, I felt betrayed by the system. I'd never felt like a victim before, but now I thought, *How could they do this to me?*

Then I went deeper. I've always thought of big obstacles in my way as giants to slay, and I realized that this was just the biggest giant I had faced yet. What did I have to do to get out of my current state of affairs? I knew I wasn't going to play the victim for long, but where to start?

The answer came on an extremely hot day a few months later. My shoulder was acting up, so I worked all day with a wrap holding my arm to my side. After work I was driving to get my weekly chiropractic adjustment when my Jeep broke down. I was fed up! I one-arm pushed my Jeep to the side of the road, then walked the two miles to my chiropractor's office. When I sat down, my first thought was, *Wow, this guy gets to work in air conditioning. He gets to help people, nobody's yelling at him and he works with his hands all day. Maybe I could do this.*

Part of me thought, *Yeah, maybe I could!* But I was scared. I'd never been a good student, and here I was thinking I could become a doctor.

I thought about it for a while, then I found a pen and, on the back of a magazine, I wrote down the three main things I realized that I, or anyone, needed to do in order to overcome their fears:

- **Show up.** Face your fears and confront what lies ahead.
- **Have a vision.** See the target you're striving for.
- **Believe.** Success starts with believing in yourself.

After the appointment, my fiancée arrived to pick me up. I said, "Sweetheart, I'm going back to school to become a doctor!"

Annette looked at me and said, "Great! What do we need to do?"

I was ready with the first step. "Show up! Step up!" I told her that the first thing I had to do was show up and accept the challenge. Someone once said that the person with the most certainty wins, and another said that if you can muster up 20 seconds of courage, you can accomplish anything. Standing in front of any fear and facing it head-on is the first step in conquering it. And I was certain I could do that.

On the way home, I told Annette that the second step I had to take was to set a vision, a target. Where am I going? I needed to get clear on that. And the third thing was to believe that I can do it. And do it great.

Before I tell you what happened, let's take a look at these three "giant-slayers."

Giant-Slayer #1: Face Your Fear

Check in with yourself now. Do you have a giant you're facing? Will you give your very best every time you stand in front of your fear? Any time I find myself standing in a tough spot, I remind myself that I am in the right place at the right time. Maybe I'm in a scary situation or a slump at this moment, but I remind myself to look at the mountain's peaks and the valleys, and ask, "Where does everything grow?"

The answer? "Down in the valleys." So maybe being down in a valley is not such a bad thing sometimes.

When things don't look so great, I trust that something good will come from the situation. I can look back and see that there were great lessons for me in those down moments. So, now I choose to be okay with them as they're happening. This is my life. It's what's happening right now. And I can't change what has been put before me, but I *can* choose how I feel, think and act about it. I can turn and run, or stand and slay my giant.

Have one thing in mind when facing your fears: success! Own it. I will conquer this. When you can see where you want to go, you know that even the giants in your path are helping you on your way. Remember that things only happen *for* you—not *to* you.

Giant-Slayer #2: Clarify Your Vision

Once you've faced your giants, you need to take the second step and get clear on your vision. To attain the things that you desire most in this world, you have to have a vision of what that looks like and believe that you have the power to create it.

So, first, you have to see the goal clearly in your heart and mind. And I mean crystal clear. Your vision is your target, your dream, your passion—the destination at the end of the path you're walking. You can create anything you can imagine in your mind. With your thoughts, you're creating the story of your life every day, and you have the ability to make anything happen.

Gandhi said, "Keep your thoughts positive, because your thoughts become your words. Keep your words positive, because your words become your behaviors. Keep your behaviors positive, because your behaviors become your habits. Keep your habits positive, because your habits become your values. Keep your values positive, because your values become your destiny."

To help you keep your vision clearly in mind, I recommend creating a vision board, also called a dream board—a big piece of cardboard that you cover with pictures cut out of magazines of what you want to have in your life. It's very similar to writing out your goals, except that pictures evoke more emotion than words on a page do. This difference has proven to make vision boards a more powerful tool for me and many others.

Put your vision board someplace where you'll see it every day, and spend at least five minutes every morning and every night before bed looking at it. Take your time and feel the emotions that each picture is evoking in you. Notice the colors on your board, and be sure they're ones that stimulate and inspire your creative center. Notice the energy you feel when you look at all the wonderful places you'll be going and things you'll be enjoying.

You have to have a clear target in front of you to know where you're going. If you don't, you're destined to be lost! And when obstacles show up, remember that everything happens for a reason, even though we often don't know what it is. We have to face what's happening right now, even while holding on to our vision.

I was in Jackson Hole snowboarding recently, and my friends and I came across the "tree runs," areas where there are no trails, just trees and empty spaces, and you have to find your way through. I had two choices: focus on avoiding the trees or on finding the open spaces between them. Fortunately, I quickly learned to focus on where I wanted to go—the open spaces. Because if you stare at a tree long enough, you're going to hit it!

Your body will follow the thoughts and beliefs that are running in your subconscious mind. Thoughts of doubts and fears have never accomplished anything, and never will. Powerful thinking ceases when doubts and fears creep in, and dwelling on them will only lead to failure, which is not an option.

I have just one option that I allow in, and that is success, so I keep the goal in sight at all times. This isn't easy because the path is scattered with distractions and obstacles, some hidden like the limbs and roots hiding under the snow even in the open spaces on the mountain. Just like them, your doubts and fears are disintegrating elements that break up the vision and steer you off path.

Life throws us obstacles frequently, but it's how we respond to them that is key. Hence, the importance of looking at your vision board at least twice daily. You have to keep your eye on the desired path. Remember, the key point of "The Star-Spangled Banner" was *seeing* "that our flag was still there." Never forget that as long as you can see your vision in your mind's eye, there is hope that you'll achieve it.

And that leads us to the last requirement.

Giant-Slayer #3: Believe in Yourself

You have to believe you're going to achieve your vision, and you have to *expect* it, or something better, to happen at the appropriate time. There's an old saying: "If you think you can, you're right, and if you think you can't, you're also right." Your life is the way it is because of your beliefs. What are your beliefs? Just look around you and you'll see what they are. If you don't have what you want yet, you don't believe you deserve it yet.

Sometimes we think we have one set of beliefs, when in actuality we're being run by others that are stored deep in our subconscious mind. You can see what your true beliefs are just by looking at your life because your subconscious mind is constantly sending out a signal that attracts more of the same kind of energy. The frequency you're tuned in to subconsciously, whether positive or negative, will always attract experiences of that same frequency back to you.

I read about an elderly woman who lived in a high-rise condo building in the city and was deathly afraid of someone breaking into her home and robbing her. She was extra cautious and had multiple locks and a security system in her home. Then, one night her condo—and only her condo—was broken into. Coincidence? Bad luck? Or a case of what you think about, you bring about?

Your beliefs act like an antenna. They allow you to receive experiences that match the frequency you are subconsciously emitting 24 hours a day, 7 days a week, 365 days a year. Each channel that we dial in to will give us experiences that match it—whether good or bad!

Our beliefs need to be updated periodically as time goes on. We have to analyze them to find out which ones are actually truthful, which ones are empowering and fulfilling, and which ones are limiting or not in sync with our thoughts or actions. You can assess your beliefs by the way the world is unfolding around you. The world as you see it is the result of what you believe.

I was in chiropractic school when I heard Dr. Morter say those words: "What you think about, you bring about." He went on to say that every thought we have reaches into the heavens and prepares a path for us, a path that allows us to have the experiences that will mold us into the people who stand looking in the mirror today. Often we don't have a clue as to who that person is. We wonder, *How did I get here? Am I a victim of my life, or am I the creator of my life?*

I believe we are the creators, and we call in the perfect experiences to mold us into exactly the person we are meant to become. Some experiences may be painful, some may be joyful and some might be expensive. But I believe that the experiences you have are all there for you to learn from. They are never against you. They are all perfect for you. You're actually in the right place, right now, having the perfect moment—whether you're liking it or not.

You just have to follow these three simple steps (simple but not always easy!), and you can accomplish anything:

- **Show up** with more power than the giant in front of you.
- **Keep your vision** in your heart, mind and sight. Create your vision board. Look at it daily. And start today.
- **Believe** that you will succeed.

I've trained all of my patients over the past twenty years to use these principles, and I've witnessed thousands of miracles. Do you want to create a miracle in your life? Join me in this endeavor. Let's all stand in the face of every giant with certainty, with vision and with strong belief in ourselves, and soon we will all stand in a better world.

Dr. Jim Claussen is not your everyday chiropractor. His alternative approach to patient care extends beyond the needs of the body to also include the needs of the mind and soul. With over 20 years of studying and learning from experts all over the world, Dr. Jim provides whole-person care for each of his patients. Through the use of chiropractic techniques, muscle-response testing and hands-on, non-forceful energy-balancing procedures, Dr. Jim brings a

deeper level of healing and consciousness by reestablishing the full healing potential of the body.

Dr. Jim lives in the western Chicago suburbs with his wife, Annette, and their five daughters. He enjoys being physically active playing golf, snowboarding and wake surfing. Visit Dr. Jim's website at drclaussen.com.

Chapter 28

Spread Your Wings like a SWAN:
Four Essential Elements of Nurturing Yourself

Carol McNulty-Huffman

W hat?!" I screamed, as I reviewed our upcoming family travel schedule. "We're staying in nine different places in seventeen days?!"

Once it was all down on paper it looked impossible. How would I ever stay healthy on such a trip and still enjoy this precious time with my family? My husband, my daughter and I were embarking on a trip to visit over 35 family members, and I was really looking forward to it. But to make this trip work and be enjoyable, and to not get sick along the way as I had on previous trips, I knew that it was essential that I nurture myself. I knew I needed to find a way to adapt my home self-care habits to traveling if I was going to stay healthy and happy enough to "shine my light" (my favorite image for my number-one goal in life) wherever I went!

Over the next few days, as I pondered how to take care of myself on this trip, I was transported back to the time and place where I actually got started on the

209

path of better self-care. In 1981, I worked at Biscayne National Park in South Florida as a park ranger and environmental education coordinator. The job consisted of taking school children camping and leading boat tours and water activities like snorkeling for the general public, and I loved it.

That summer, the park staff was in the midst of eradicating alien tree species, especially the Brazilian Pepper (*Schinus terebinthifolius*), so the park's native hardwood hammock could thrive again. One day, I decided that the Schinus tree in my front yard had to go too, so I cut it down with a hacksaw and carried the wood and branches to the dumpster. A few days later, I broke out in an itchy, oozy, crusty rash on the front of my arms and legs. Yikes! I later learned that this tree sometimes causes a poison ivy–type rash in sensitive individuals like me. The upside was that the pain and discomfort of that time started me on a lifelong journey of healing—physically at first, with emotional, mental and spiritual healing to follow.

In the process, I learned to take excellent care of myself and, especially, to love myself more. Isn't that the heart of self-care? Loving yourself enough to know you are truly worth taking care of exquisitely well.

On my spiritual journey, I came to believe that we are all individual expressions of the One Universal Life-Force Energy I call God, or Loving Spirit, or Love-Intelligence—there are so many possible names. I believe that all life has, at its core, a Divine seed that seeks expression, and that our self-care is a reflection of how much we love ourselves and our Creator. Caring for ourselves and others is ultimately an act of reverence for life itself.

I recalled these values as I focused on my current dilemma of fitting in adequate self-care on our upcoming trip. Meditation, prayer and journaling are my favorite avenues for problem solving, so I started there, and as soon as I took time to get quiet and clear, answers came. Out of these answers, I developed simple self-care strategies that allowed me to honor myself and at the same time be fully present with everyone we visited along the way.

I sat with journal in hand and focused on the big picture by asking myself, *What key elements will enable me to stay healthy and happy on this trip?* I came up with four—adequate sleep, good nutrition, clean water and healthy air. Then, for each one, I drilled down to the details of how I would make it happen.

Before long, the details started to overwhelm me. I couldn't get them down on paper fast enough, and I wondered how I would ever remember them. I knew it was time to pause, release my mental effort and let the answers simply come. I love to set myself up for solutions to come effortlessly, so I went to bed and let my subconscious mind work on the answers while I slept.

Each night when I get into bed, I like to turn my thoughts to how I would like the next day to flow. As I drift off to sleep, I remind myself that I am sleeping deeply and waking refreshed, joyous, clear and energetic—and I do wake that way most of the time these days, even on limited sleep. This is a much better approach than my old way of lying in bed, chiding myself for getting to bed too late and worrying about how tired I'd be in the morning. Because, guess what, staying awake worrying *did* make me tired the next day! It was like the old adage, "Whether you think you can or think you can't, you're right!"

Some nights, I specify the knowledge, or insight, I want to gain by morning— in fact, this is one of my favorite healthy, multitasking endeavors. That night, I stated specifically that I wanted to come up with an easy way to remember how to take good care of myself. When I woke up the next morning, I was mentally playing with the first letter of each area of concern: sleep, nutrition, water and air. I noticed that, in a different order, they spelled the word "swan." *Aha!* I thought. *That's easy to remember!*

So, I'd like to share with you the four elements of SWAN—standing for Sleep, Water, Air and Nutrition—and the strategies I developed to manage each one in my self-care routine on our trip. Also, in case you're wondering, I did encourage my husband and daughter to join me in these strategies, but I made sure I didn't nag them about it and we all got along great, having one of our best trips ever!

Sleep

Volumes have been written on the value of sleep and its importance to your health. I Googled "the value of a good night's sleep" and got 11 million hits! Experts agree that healthy sleep habits are essential for a good quality of life and also to promote longevity and healthy aging. I imagine you're all too well aware of the effects of getting inadequate sleep for a day or two, including tiredness, brain fog, impaired response time, sluggish bodily functions and attention difficulties.

When this turns into chronic sleep deprivation, things get more serious and stressful. Scientists have now shown us that long-term lack of sleep (defined as even just one week of fewer than six hours a night) is detrimental to your health and includes such impacts as increased inflammation, a revved-up stress response and impaired metabolism. I learned that sleep and metabolism are controlled by the same center of the brain, and that people who are sleep-deprived have a greater propensity toward heart disease, stroke, arthritis, depression, diabetes and obesity.

Getting a good night's sleep on a consistent basis was even more important than I had known. So, how did I plan for that on our trip?

First, when possible, I arranged for our travel to begin midmorning, not at the crack of dawn! Then, when considering the leg of the trip from Hawaii to the eastern continental United States, we elected to spend one night in California rather than push through and get to our destination in one day.

I also set firm family boundaries on how late I would go touring or stay up visiting. As each day began, I checked on how early we needed to be up the next day, so that I could plan the best time to return to our lodging and get to bed. When I first proposed this boundary to my husband and daughter, they reacted strongly. I held my ground but gave them the freedom to explore during my downtimes, and it all worked out well.

Keeping this boundary was especially tough in New York City. After a full day of touring and being stimulated by the sights and sounds of the city, including art museums, a Broadway play, subway rides and culturally diverse food, even I could easily have kept going. But I knew that I, and all of us, would pay for it if we did, and we all ended up glad we hadn't let ourselves overdo it.

In the evening, I used my standard approaches to supporting sleep, including low lighting starting an hour before bedtime and sleeping in total darkness. I got extra towels to put over the various clocks and light switches and used a little white noise machine to drown out hotel and street noise. I also took a supplement containing melatonin to help me reset my body's clock in each new time zone.

In our travel schedule, I carved out time for seven to eight hours of sleep, as well as two hours to wind down in the evening and two hours to get up and get ready for the day. If we were scheduled to travel to a new place that day, I gave myself an extra hour to get organized and pack for the next leg of our travels.

I did this even if I had to pull myself away from family fun and connection time, another toughie. I found that everyone we visited was very understanding; some of them were even relieved that this gave them extra space, too!

Water

We all know how essential drinking enough good, clean water is to a healthy life. When I'm well hydrated, I simply feel better. I've also known the debilitating effects of dehydration, which are magnified at medium to high elevations and can include nausea, dry skin, constipation, headaches and fatigue.

Why is dehydration more severe at elevation? Humidity is lower at higher altitudes and sweat evaporates more quickly, so you may not realize how much water you're losing, even with little exertion. With the lower oxygen levels at higher elevations, you also breathe in and out faster, causing you to lose more water through respiration.

Did you know that air travel is like taking your body to about 10,000 feet? This means it's especially helpful to stay hydrated while flying. A good guide for air travel is to drink twice as much as you drink at sea level; for me that means drinking 16 ounces an hour, rather than my normal eight.

When traveling, I use bottled water, and if that's not available, I boil the water to remove the chlorine. Upon arriving at a new place, I put water first on our list of supplies to gather, so that it will be available the next morning.

My first health habit of the day, wherever I am, is drinking warm water! Not only does it begin to hydrate your cells, it also wakes up your digestive and elimination systems. For the trip, I carried a thermos and filled it with eight ounces of hot water before bed. In the morning, it was the perfect temperature to drink. I also generally bring a travel heating element along, just in case there's no way to boil water.

Air

Out on the road, particles too tiny to see with the naked eye are released into the air from trucks, cars, factories and power plants. When we breathe these particles deep into the lungs, they can irritate the tissue and cause inflammation. Such exposure increases an individual's risk of asthma, stroke, heart attack and other serious illnesses.

Depending on where you live, you may have higher or lower exposure to air pollutants when you travel.

I find the gas fumes that enter airplanes at the beginning and end of a flight particularly challenging. In seeking solutions, I found a small, portable fresh-air diffuser that I keep in my carry-on bag. It fits in the palm of my hand, and when I notice fumes or other irritating odors, I simply hold the diffuser close to my nose. I also travel with a small portable air purifier that I set up, as needed, wherever we stay. Some hotels offer purified rooms for sensitive guests, and I reserve those when possible.

Nutrition

The Center for Science in the Public Interest indicates that poor nutrition reduces our quality of life and can even shorten it. Unhealthy eating, along with physical inactivity, is actually a leading cause of death in the United States. Over two-thirds of American adults are overweight or obese, and the rates of diet-related diseases—such as heart disease, stroke, cancer and diabetes—are on the rise. So, getting good nutrition is always essential, even when you're traveling. This area involves the most prep work beforehand, but when I take the time to do it, I'm always so glad I did.

First on my nutrition travel list are packets I make up that provide greens, protein and fiber all at once. I mix green powder, ground chia and rice protein in little plastic zipper bags, making one for each day. Just mix with water for a refreshing and power-packed drink. I also travel with my daily supplements, healthy snacks (almonds, especially), extra rice protein powder and a quick breakfast (needed about 50 percent of the time), usually whole-grain instant oats or a bagel. My favorite tip, though, is to carry a bottle of avocado oil and some sea salt to use on salads when healthy oils aren't available.

After I start each day with eight ounces of warm water, I follow that soon after with tea and fruit. I get dressed and ready for the day and then drink my green drink. It's great to know that I'm already certain of good nutrition and hydration, no matter how the day rolls. I sometimes create an AM bag, a daily bag and a PM bag for my various nutritional components.

Throughout the trip, I found that it was easy to simply review the word SWAN twice a day and quickly run through each element to see if it was covered. If I had the element handled, great! If not, I had simple action steps ready to make it happen.

And there you have it—the four basic elements of self-care I use to nurture myself, so I can stay happy, healthy and more easily able to shine my light, whether on a trip or anywhere else I happen to find myself. Your top elements may be different than mine; surely there are many more to include, such as sunlight, silence, work, attitude, activity and non-activity, to name just a few that fit the SWAN acronym.

I trust my story will inspire you to use or adapt these strategies to suit your needs and make the vitally important job of nurturing yourself easier than ever before. Above all, know thyself, and create a system that works for you. After all, you deserve to spread your wings like a swan, so you can travel far and shine your light wherever you go!

Carol McNulty-Huffman is a writer and inspirational speaker and the founder of Wellspring Empowerment Enterprises, LLC. She lives on the island of Maui in Hawaii. Earlier in life, she had an adventurous career as a park ranger, serving as a guide and natural resource manager in six different national parks. She also spent six years as a park planner. Her professional life, however, didn't prepare her for the birth of her special needs daughter. There was no guide and no plan, and there were no apparent resources. The

life-changing journey of transforming the stress and struggle of her experience into the gift of a lifetime is the subject of her upcoming book, The Art of Ease and Grace. *For a free experience of Carol's favorite balancing meditation, please visit www. theartofeaseandgrace.com/meditation.*

Chapter 29 ---

The Surprising Secret to Success
in the Workplace: Love
Magnes Welsh

T he man on the stage said, "All emotions boil down to either love or fear," and I felt like I'd been hit by a lightning bolt. The words sent an electrical charge through me, a charge that cracked me open and changed my view of life forever.

With that one sentence, the late Wayne Dyer showed me that everything that isn't love is just another name for fear. Anger. Criticism. Disappointment and sadness. Feeling "not good enough." Seeking perfection. All are fundamentally feelings of fear. And once I saw that, I could see how fear ruled so much of my life and the lives of many others around me, and often served as our motivator.

It had taken me more than 20 years to truly understand that my drive to succeed in business was motivated by fear. I saw it most clearly in my harsh judgment of my own behavior and others'. This came naturally to me, having been a child of the 1950s. My parents, particularly my mother, were full of fears, the causes ranging from monthly bills to health scares (such as polio) to the menace of the Cold War. We lived in our own box of fears as a staunch Roman Catholic family in Memphis, Tennessee, with plenty of judgments about other people and about ourselves.

In an effort to make my sister and me better people, my parents used rearing techniques that relied heavily on pointing out shortcomings and trying not to overdo praise for what we did well. Being good and doing well was expected—no extra credit for that! For example, Mother responded to a report card of As and Bs with a stern "I expect straight As. You can do it. Just do more homework."

This was actually excellent training for the constant pressure of the "More! Better! Faster!" attitude at the companies where I now worked. But what kind of life does that really prepare you for? Where is the joy and fulfillment in it?

As I listened to Dyer that evening and reflected on his words in the following months, many questions came up. Was he saying that fear wasn't necessary? Was there another choice, and was it something as pleasant as love? We all value love, but could it ever work in the workplace?

I had just started my own consulting business in public relations and communications after more than 15 years of working at FedEx and in senior management at Kraft, Inc. And, as Dyer's words sank in deeper, more and more of my hidden, or disguised, fears about work surfaced. In the weeks and months to follow, I began to realize how unloving I was to myself. I was beating myself up almost daily with negative thoughts about the smallest things and always trying to do things "perfectly." I was clearly my own worst critic.

So, I started to be more compassionate with myself and to shift my thoughts—even saying "I'm sorry" to myself in a loving way when I lapsed into negative self-talk. And since my career was an important and exciting part of my life, I experimented with similar practices at work.

My first major effort was with a client company that was proving to be difficult after having hired me to start a media relations program for them. I thought, *Why not see if my new ways of quiet compassion and love would work in the business world?*

For 10 years prior to my arrival, the client's normal operating procedure had been basically to avoid the press, so I went into this assignment with my eyes open to the challenges. After "get acquainted" meetings with reporters from a number of major publications, the CEO complained that one reporter wore tennis shoes, another wasn't "sharp," and a third "didn't understand our business." I saw the fear behind all this faultfinding, but it was hard at first to know how to address it.

The last straw was the day the CEO said he didn't think *The Wall Street Journal* reporter covering his industry was smart. At that point, I seriously considered firing this client. It seemed hopeless! But talk about a frightening thought. My business was only three years old, and firing one of my few clients was uncharted territory.

I knew I needed a deeper insight into the situation, so that weekend I decided to be silent to see what bubbled up in me: no reading, no television, no computers, no calling my friends and family. I rested, did minor chores around my condo, asked for wisdom and listened.

Nothing came.

And then, at about 3:00 PM on Sunday, all of a sudden a lightbulb switched on in my head. Instantly, I "saw" my own arrogance about this company, which was a partnership, not a public company, and much smaller than my former employer. I saw my critical feelings, ranging from *How dare they think major newspapers and magazines are going to magically jump to write about them!* to *They certainly have an inflated view of their firm.* I also saw that I was heaping judgments and criticism on them because I feared that they could make *me* look bad. No wonder they were fearful and distrusting around me!

To my surprise, once I had this wake-up call and saw my own fear and arrogance about the client, *their* behavior changed almost immediately. No one said that a reporter was dumb or doing a bad job again, and I realized that those responses must have been a reflection of my own negative feelings. Within a few weeks, there was a new wave of cooperation among the company's senior leaders, myself and the reporters.

And then another insight came in a planning meeting a few months later. The CEO and other executives were basically ignoring the communications plan they were there to review, and I was getting aggravated. As an experiment, I shifted my feelings from being irritated with the group to sending them positive energy by opening my heart. I intentionally felt warm, loving energy inside myself and then felt it circulating around them. Within 10 minutes, they turned their attention to the plan and focused on it, and within another 15 minutes, they had agreed to it with minor adjustments.

Had the loving energy really worked? Was it magic? I was shocked by how fast things had changed. But as I tested this "technique" over time, I saw that the effect it had was real. When I felt loving energy during interviews we had with reporters, the CEO delivered his messages well, the reporters' coverage was more accurate and everyone was happier. Make that *much* happier! It ultimately led to successes with all the media campaigns we launched. Over time, my responsibilities grew and their media coverage increased significantly because of the growth of the company.

Since those days, I've made this a frequent practice with other clients with consistently near-miraculous results. It's easy! And so much more rewarding than wasting time fuming in silence or complaining later to my colleagues.

So, I invite you to take a moment to consider: How often do you criticize yourself? Maybe for how you look? How you performed on a project? What you said in a meeting? Even for switching lanes in traffic and choosing a slower one? And how often do you criticize others, thinking you know better? We are so often unconsciously unloving toward ourselves and others, and I believe that's the root of almost any failure we might have in life. Our thoughts and emotions are far more powerful than we commonly recognize.

For example, have you ever felt that you were being stabbed, yet there were no knives in sight? It was probably from your own or someone else's negative thoughts. I call it an "energetic attack." Someone else can "stab" you, and we also do it to ourselves and to those around us. But whatever the kind of attack, the ultimate and unfailing defense is the same: to shift back to positive, loving, compassionate thoughts and feelings about ourselves and others. In this incredibly simple way, we are each truly invincible.

Some years later, a different challenge arose at this company. The head of marketing told me that a key financial executive didn't think I was very smart. I had received criticisms in my career, but that was a new one. Normally, I would have taken offense, but this time I took a few quiet minutes to intentionally start opening my heart, and then I sent this man positive energy.

I continued to do so at every opportunity in the following days and months, and it worked. The feeling from him shifted, and we worked together on half a dozen acquisitions and then on taking this private company through an initial public offering to be listed on the New York Stock Exchange. There were plenty of tense meetings with the bankers and various groups during this process, but they just gave me more opportunities to expand my experiments of sending positive energy, and these activities were successful and mostly harmonious.

A particularly difficult test came later during merger proceedings with a global company based in London. The deal was called off a few times due to various stumbling blocks, and I stopped counting the rewrites after 25 drafts of the main announcement (a record never equaled in my career). In my eyes, the CEO of the other company was a major stumbling block because he would agree to something and then change his mind. But I chose to send him love instead of negative energy, and slowly he became more supportive.

My practice of generating love was my normal operating procedure throughout this process, and there were so many players and so many opportunities for conflict that it was a great proving ground. And what a success it was! Eleven months later, the merger was finally announced in France at a huge international industry meeting. Thanks to the media plan having been refined so many times and all the key reporters attending the meeting, the plan was executed virtually flawlessly. The merger provided actual news to report, and everyone was full of smiles due to the positive coverage. By the end, the small group of us from both companies who had worked in secrecy had a close-knit alliance.

And remember the man who said I wasn't smart? He was a key architect of the merger, and he shocked me by naming me and four other people at the first joint meeting of the combined company's senior leaders. He thanked us for our tremendous support and for being steadfast, patient partners throughout the protracted process. I was the only consultant he mentioned.

This habit of using love to smooth the way is really an inside job. The only person you can ever change is yourself, so practice finding love daily for yourself, as well as for those you're dealing with. At a certain point, I had to really discipline myself to break the deep-seated habit of focusing on negative thoughts and shift to positive ones. But it was well worth the effort. It's so rewarding to release your unloving feelings and relearn how to love yourself (warts and all), as well as each person and perceived obstacle in your life.

Remembering to love myself unconditionally is a journey that continues to this day. And, after more than 25 years and plenty of slipups along the way, my suggestion is to take it one day at a time and see that the challenges, setbacks and, yes, even the rejections are all just as perfect as the successes. Be patient with yourself and others because, deep down, everyone is looking for harmony and success—even though many certainly don't seem to be.

I believe each person and each situation in life offers us a gift: the chance to stretch to find the love and expand to become a bigger person, no matter how disappointing or challenging the circumstances. The trick is to recognize that gift and accept it—and that isn't always easy. Some of my biggest gifts have come at what seemed like the bleakest times when it was hard to see clearly past hurtful actions and my own or others' negative emotions. But it's worth it. A couple of my clients regularly say they hope to reincarnate to have my life because it does seem to be charmed. With some, I share that there were many struggles to get to this place, but all the credit goes to my discovery that the surest path to success is shifting from judgment and fear to love and positivity.

Traveling this road will create an ever happier and more successful life, and sometimes even immediate results. Since the night of that wake-up call from Wayne Dyer in an auditorium of 400 people, my life has gotten better and better, and my professional success has grown steadily—and I believe you'll see the same results if you try this simple practice. Like me, you might find that little miracles occur often as your love grows and your challenges start melting away into blessings. This human life is a multifaceted, exciting journey and a joyful one, I promise you, if you use love as your compass to navigate it.

Magnes Welsh is the author of the book The Art and Heart of Business, *which grew out of her passion for replacing fear with love in the workplace. In the book, she makes the case for the business benefits of shifting to love, and also reveals simple practices she developed over 25 years in her independent consultancy, Magnes Communications.*

A communications expert, Magnes has more than 35 years' experience in bringing strategy and clarity to messaging, crisis management and reporting for corporations and nonprofit organizations, including FedEx and Kraft Foods, where she served as director of public relations. She also has expertise in sustainability and social responsibility from her work with multinational companies, such as Chiquita Brands International. She earned an MBA with honors from the Kellogg School of Management at Northwestern University and is a certified keynote speaker. To learn more about The Art and Heart of Business, *go to MagnesWelsh.com.*

Chapter 30

How to Shine Your Light
Geoff Affleck

When it's said and done,
You know in your heart
That your song is sung.
Don't go with your song still inside you.
Let it guide you every day.
We all know that it's good to be humble, but don't grumble your life away.
—**Ethan Lipton** and **Christopher Ferreira**, "Song Inside"

How about you? Do you have a song still inside you—a message to share with others that you just know needs to be birthed?

Imagine how you would feel at the end of your life if your song wasn't sung and the message you were born to share never reached the people that it could have helped the most.

I'm sure you've noticed how passionate my co-authors are about their messages and what a difference their advice has made to themselves and others.

What about you? What message or idea lights you up? What wisdom or advice do you have to offer?

I believe that there's a reason many of us were born into challenging circumstances, or endured dramatic or painful experiences that shaped our lives, and that all of us are blessed with unique talents, skills and gifts and have passions that we want to pursue and share. And, of course, that reason is so that we can help others to overcome similar challenges. It's up to us whether we sing our song or leave this earth with our song still inside us. It's a choice.

As for me, I don't consider myself to be a self-help guru. I don't have a transformational message to share that will uplift or inspire thousands of people, and there are no processes, methods or seven-step systems that I teach. Although I haven't invented a new technique for improving one's health, relationships or finances, I'm blessed to have had a significant role in impacting the lives of countless people who are suffering or feel lost, or who are challenged by life's circumstances or simply want to become a better version of themselves. How do I do that? Simply by helping those teachers and experts who have the answers to these complex life problems reach the people they are meant to reach.

My motivation for writing this chapter is to share with you my best practical advice for reaching the people for whom you are meant to "sing your song." But first let me share a little of my journey…

From Ski Instructor to Marketing Consultant

As a young adult, my passion was downhill skiing. For 25 years, I shared my love of the sport, first as a ski instructor and later as co-owner and co-director of Toronto's oldest ski and snowboard school for children—a business my wife, Lesley, and I ran together. After growing that business for six years, we sold it for a tidy profit, and I went into semi-retirement for two years before feeling called to share my business management skills with other entrepreneurs.

"My business is an absolute mess!" confided my friend Warren, a creator of beautiful hand-carved and hand-illustrated cedar signs. Warren was a true artist, whose signs adorned the storefronts and driveways of many businesses and homes in his idyllic West Coast hometown and as far away as Europe. As with many "right-brained" entrepreneurs, business management and marketing were not his passions, skills or talents.

Warren's record-keeping is almost nonexistent (a bunch of receipts and bills stuffed in drawers). Sales were hemorrhaging. His energy was scattered, as he jumped from one thing to the next throughout each 12-hour workday. The 20-year-old yellow shag carpet in his home office was toxic, and an ad in the Yellow Pages was his marketing plan!

"Let me help you," I offered. And so began my first small-business makeover more than 10 years ago. The first phase was to create a healthy work environment by tearing up the toxic carpet (I did home makeovers back then as well as business makeovers). Next, we set up the quoting, invoicing, bookkeeping and accounting systems. The third phase focused on marketing, including raising his prices and launching a new website.

Warren was thrilled with the results and I discovered a new passion: helping entrepreneurs reach more people with their products, services and information. I called my new company "Small Business Makeovers."

Since then I've had the good fortune to learn from, and work alongside, some brilliant mentors, including *New York Times* bestselling authors T. Harv Eker, Janet Bray Attwood, Chris Attwood and Marci Shimoff.

Chris, Janet and Marci introduced me to the world of personal growth programs, workshops and books. Together, for the past five years, through our Enlightened Bestseller program, we've mentored hundreds of aspiring self-help authors (including all of the contributing authors to this book) to navigate the rapidly changing world of writing, publishing and marketing their transformational messages.

I'm so proud of so many of our students who've gone on to change thousands of lives by writing #1 bestselling books, launching online courses, becoming sought-after speakers and leading empowering live events.

How about you? Is it your turn to shine your light a little brighter?

Let me share this simple, practical exercise with you to get started.

Preparing to Shine Your Light

The common purpose we all share is to serve each other. You will be successful when you find ways to combine your natural talents, your learned skills, your life experiences and your passions in a way that solves a problem or fulfills a critical need for others. Use the following worksheet to help clarify exactly how you will do that.

Part 1:

1. What are your natural **talents**? A talent is your God-given natural ability to do something. What things come naturally to you? List five of your talents here:

   i. _____

   ii. _____

   iii. _____

   iv. _____

   v. _____

2. What are your **skills**? A skill is a proficiency at something, usually acquired by putting in a lot of time and effort to learn it. List five of your skills here:

   i. _____

   ii. _____

   iii. _____

   iv. _____

   v. _____

3. What remarkable **experiences,** challenging life circumstances, traumatic events, turnarounds and successes have you had that have impacted your life? List up to five of them here:

   i. _____

   ii. _____

   iii. _____

   iv. _____

   v. _____

4. What are your **passions**? A passion is defined as a strong feeling of enthusiasm or excitement for something. I recommend taking *The Passion Test* every year to get clear on your top five passions (Learn more at www.thepassiontest.com). List your top five passions here:

i. _____

ii. _____

iii. _____

iv. _____

v. _____

Part 2:

Drawing on one to three items from each of your lists above, fill in the blanks below:

By sharing my natural TALENTS for _____

_____

_____

and my learned SKILLS of _____

_____

_____

and my life EXPERIENCES of _____

_____

_____

I will share my PASSIONS for _____

_____

_____

by SERVING (Describe the type of people you want to help, such as single moms, men over 50, overweight teens.) _____

_____

_____

by helping them to solve the PROBLEM of (Write down the *specific* problem that your advice is the answer to.) _____

_____

In case you're unsure about how to do the exercise, here's an example of a completed worksheet:

By sharing my natural TALENTS for *teaching, writing, intuition and empathy;* my learned SKILLS of *psychology, counseling and public speaking;* and my life EXPERIENCES of *being a child of divorced parents and saving my own marriage in the face of divorce,* I will share my PASSION for *saving relationships* by SERVING *married couples in crisis* by helping them to solve the PROBLEM of *being in a relationship that's broken and heading for divorce.*

Now go back and read the statement you wrote and see if you can tighten it up, using the above example as a guide.

Congratulations! You now have created a mission statement to guide you as you prepare to shine your light.

I have a confession to make.

In 2012, when Janet, Chris and Marci invited me to co-facilitate the Enlightened Bestseller program with them, I didn't know much about how to market self-help books. I knew how to grow an email list and market online courses and workshops but not books.

My early mentor, T. Harv Eker, taught me a concept that I've applied often. He explained that you don't have to be an expert before you can teach others—you just have to know more than they do.

This is the approach I took when the opportunity came up to work alongside Janet, Chris and Marci. On a scale of 1 to 10, I may have been at a "level four" when I co-facilitated our first workshop. I knew I wasn't an expert, but I knew I knew enough to be of service to people. As Harv says, "Ready. Fire. Aim!"

Over the next year I studied the work of book-marketing experts to develop my skills and knowledge and began to share that knowledge with our students.

The next step was to put the knowledge I'd gained into practice, so I took the lead role in writing and publishing an ebook on the subject called *Enlightened Bestseller: 7 Keys to Creating a Successful Self-Help Book.* The ebook became a #1 bestseller and has been downloaded by thousands of aspiring authors, and it's received excellent reviews.

As a direct result of publishing *Enlightened Bestseller*, I've been interviewed by marketing experts and have presented at live and online events on the topic. And because of that ebook, I'm able to earn a living and support my family by helping others shine their light.

The concept I learned from Harv is simple: in order to become an authority in your field, you start by teaching and sharing with others who know less than you. If you're a level four, you can start teaching level ones, twos and threes. As you teach them you'll become a level five, and then you can teach up to level four. With even more practice and training, you could rise to level seven and teach up to level six, and so on—and this is how you can begin to shine your light from whatever place you are presently at in your journey.

Next I'm going to offer you a practical and simple way to take action.

Could You Be a Bestselling Author?

If a ski instructor can become a bestselling author writing about a subject he, at first, knew nothing about, might it be possible for you to write an ebook about something you know inside out and were born to share?

I'm convinced that publishing an ebook is one of the best ways to begin to shine your light and here's why:

- **Speed:** An ebook can be written quickly: 10,000 words or so (40 pages) is easy to write in a few days or weeks. You don't need to find an agent or a publisher because Amazon will gladly publish your book around the world in just a few hours.

- **Clarity:** By writing your book, you'll gain insights, clarity and a new level of mastery around your subject. The act of writing will raise your level of confidence and authority from a "one" to a "five" or perhaps from a "five" to an "eight" out of 10.

- **Low Cost:** You can get a quality cover design for as little as $5 on sites like fiverr.com. Your major expense will be hiring an editor, and this is not the place to scrimp. Your ebook should be of the same editorial quality as a printed book. Budget $500 to $1,000 for this. Otherwise, there are no costs for publishing, printing, distribution and marketing (although you could invest in marketing, if you choose to).

- **Credibility:** What would the addition of the words "bestselling author of [insert your book title here]" on your website, bio, business card and email signature do for your career? You'll be perceived as an expert and, in turn, will attract more speaking opportunities, subscribers, clients and income.

- **List Building:** Because you can insert links into your ebook, you can leverage it to build your email list as readers click through to your website to receive additional bonuses, videos and information from you.

- **Royalities:** Unlike printed books that pay the author between 7.5 and 50 percent of the price of the book, ebook royalties are as high as 70 percent. That means you earn around $2 on a $3 ebook, and this can add up fast.

What to Write About

People sometimes ask me, "What could I possibly write about?" You should have some idea from the exercise above. What are you an expert at? What are you currently teaching or have previously taught? What are you learning right now? What have you accomplished? What are your talents and skills? What are you advocating for—such as a cause or social justice issue? What do people ask you for advice about? What challenges have you overcome in your life? What unique and interesting stories do you have to share?

Have you noticed that the word "authority" contains the word "author"? It's always interesting guiding self-publishing authors through the process when they're writing books on subjects they feel passionate about but aren't true experts in. For example, take the career nutritionist who plays golf as a hobby and writes a general book about golfing tips and wonders why people don't buy it. He would be better positioned to write a book framed as *How to Eat Right to Improve Your Golf Game,* rather than *Excel at Golf,* because the book is a natural extension of his expertise, and people will "buy" his take on the subject.

Your book will reach more readers if it solves a specific problem that people are actively seeking the answer to, such as "how to fix my marriage" or "how to cure leaky gut syndrome."

Once you've narrowed down your topic, the next step is to write your Table of Contents for about 10 chapters. Here are some approaches to help you write your chapter titles:

- **FAQs:** What are the 10 questions people ask most FREQUENTLY about your topic? Survey your target market and ask:
  — What's your number-one question about [my topic]?
  — What's your number-one problem regarding [my topic]?
- **"SAQs":** What are the 10 questions people SHOULD ask about your topic? Highlighting their importance and answering them will position you as an expert.
- **Research:** Read three to five bestselling books about your topic. Look at their Table of Contents for common themes (or use Amazon's "Look Inside" feature). Review top blogs and websites on your topic for ideas.
- **Interview Experts:** Record the interviews, then transcribe them into an ebook. Better yet, interview 10 experts and create a series of 10 ebooks!
- **Blog to Book:** Convert 20 of your best blog posts into an ebook.

My passion is to help people with a transformational message shine their light in the world by guiding them through the writing, publishing and marketing process. It's rewarding to see their books published and watch their platforms grow as they reach more people with their transformational messages and advice.

I hope this inspires you to take the first steps in that direction by publishing your own ebook, so you too can shine your light.

Geoff Affleck's passion is helping self-help authors reach more people with their message. He is an authority on ebooks and is the #1 bestselling co-author of Enlightened Bestseller: 7 Keys to Creating a Successful Self-Help Book; Breakthrough!: Inspirational Strategies for an Audaciously Authentic Life; Ready, Set, Live!: Empowering Strategies for an Enlightened Life; *and* Inspired by The Passion Test: The Power of the #1 Tool for Discovering Your Passion & Purpose.

Geoff has shared the stage with T. Harv Eker, Marci Shimoff, Janet Bray Attwood, Chris Attwood, John Assaraf and Debra Poneman. He is a certified Passion Test and Passion Test for Business facilitator, and has an MBA from the Schulich School of Business in Toronto. Born in Australia, he now lives on Vancouver Island, Canada, and enjoys yoga, sailing, carpentry and the loving support of his wife, Lesley, and daughter, Skyla. Connect with Geoff at geoffaffleck.com.

Morgan James
Speakers Group

↗ www.TheMorganJamesSpeakersGroup.com

We connect Morgan James published
authors with live and online events
and audiences whom will benefit
from their expertise.